MANCHESTER CITY
50 MEMORABLE MATCHES

By

STUART BRODKIN

Published in 2021 by G2 Entertainment
www.g2books.co.uk

ISBN (Paperback): 978-1-78281-466-5
ISBN (eBook): 978-1-78281-467-2

Written by Stuart Brodkin

Front cover design Paul Briggs

Book design Alex Young

Publishers Jules Gammond & Edward Adams

Printed and bound in the UK

CONTENTS

DEDICATION

AS I was putting the finishing touches to this book, a very dear friend of mine, David Gallick, passed away after a courageous but ultimately unavailing battle with cancer.

David wasn't a Man City fan – he was a long-standing and loyal supporter of Wolverhampton Wanderers – but unlike most football enthusiasts he showed no bias whatsoever and was always immensely appreciative of the beautiful style that the Blues had developed, particularly over the last decade or so.

I shall miss him more than words can say.

RIP David.

FOREWORD

By Mike Summerbee

I WAS delighted to be asked to write the foreword for this book which features 50 memorable Man City matches.

Every book on Manchester City is an "event", but this is especially so as it includes the time when the team and myself enjoyed great success.

Of course, we are enjoying an even greater measure of success these days under the management of the fantastic Pep Guardiola, but I think Pep would be the first to recognise the amazing work done by Joe Mercer and Malcolm Allison back in the day.

They say opposites attract – and Joe and Malcolm were certainly that. But they put together a side that played attractive football and were serial winners, much like today's City set-up.

Interestingly, the author has unearthed what might well be the first mention of my possible transfer from Swindon Town to Maine Road in 1965, so for me, it was a must-read.

I think for any City fan it's a must-read too, with a very personal take on 50 games ranging over a period of more than 60 years, which is quite a journey.

There are lots of ups and almost as many downs, but it's a fascinating trip on football's rollercoaster.

And through it all, the author's blue-blooded pedigree and that unique City sense of humour – common to all our fans – shines through.

Mike Summerbee,
Manchester, October 2021

Mike Summerbee made 357 appearances for City (1965-75), scoring 47 goals, winning four major trophies, including the European Cup Winners' Cup, in three seasons. He also played eight times for England (1968-73).

He is now a Club Ambassador at City.

Chapter 1

THE JOURNEY BEGINS

City 1 Birmingham City 1
Maine Road
First Division
Saturday, 31 March 1956
Attendance: 44,777

City: Trautmann, Leivers, Little, Barnes, Ewing, Paul, Spurdle, Hayes, Revie, Dyson, Clarke [**Hayes**]

Manager: Les McDowall

Birmingham City: Merrick, Allen, Green, Watts, Smith, Linecor, Astall, Finney, Lane, Murphy, Govan. [**Murphy**]

ACCORDING to the Chinese philosopher Lao Tzu "A journey of a thousand miles starts with a single step".

Well, Lao Tzu may have been a contemporary of Confucius, but he certainly wasn't a City fan – as far as we know!

So, let me tell you that this City-supporting journey has encompassed way more than a thousand miles although it did begin with a single step – out of my grandfather's car and into what looked to me like a vast arena, Maine Road.

My brother Adrian and I were not in double figures age-wise when our maternal grandpa, always known as 'Pap', took us to our first City game.

Pap was, shall we say, frugal, so we only saw the final ten minutes when they opened the gates to let the crowd out. We, and a few other cheapskates (although I didn't know the word at the time), were rushing in the opposite direction.

The journey had begun; it was a journey that had way more downs than ups, certainly until the last decade or so, but I wouldn't have missed it for the world.

To tell the truth I remember very little of that first taste of MCFC, admittedly not a great 'come on' for anyone who has just picked up this book and is hoping to read about all the memorable games I've seen over the years! But it does get better, I promise.

What I do remember are the sounds, smells and colours of a Maine Road crowd which overwhelmed my senses.

To put it as succinctly as possible: I was hooked. And so was my brother.

My love for City has never diminished – and never will. Not even when United totally dominated the football world; not even when Peter Swales ruled the roost; not even when the Francis Lee-Alan Ball axis was running the club; not even when the less-than-savoury Thaksin Shinawatra bought us out. And certainly not when Abu Dhabi United Group stepped in and bought the club from the last-named.

That's why I was so angry when Colin Shindler, who published *Manchester City Ruined My Life* in 2012, is wheeled out from time to time by one of the newspapers to rail about how Abu Dhabi has destroyed his club; a club he says he now loathes.

Of course, I get all the concerns about the human rights record of the Abu Dhabi regime and the possibility that they are using MCFC for "sportswashing" – whatever that might mean – but to say the club is now loathsome is plain wrong in my view.

Five years on from the Aguerooo moment against QPR in 2012 and not long after the Guardiola era began, Shindler told *The Independent*: "We are just part of some sort of global attempt at world domination.

"These people want a club in New York, they want a club in Melbourne. We are not Manchester City; we just happen to be their club in England that's part of a portfolio.

"It's like the Chrysler Building – getting a new centre half is like re-fitting the air-conditioning in the Chrysler Building.

"The sense of emotional identification with the players and the fans is what I miss most about the old era.

"I have no interest in any of these players – I admire Silva and Aguero, but they're not Colin Bell.

"I'm completely out of sympathy with where football is going. I claim nothing original about what I'm saying, but what I won't do is join in with the general cause of saying 'isn't the Premier League wonderful?' I don't believe it.

"I'm perfectly happy to stick my head above the parapet and say I loathe what's happened to my club, I loathe the people in charge of my club.

"The feeling of oneness with the club is never going to come back. The identification with Manchester has gone.

"I have fond memories of fanatical devotion to a club which doesn't exist anymore.

"Colin Bell was my hero and Mike Summerbee was my hero – these are heroic characters you can relate to. I always liked the local nature of football."

Emotive words, for sure, but not the words of a true fan – and remember, fan is an abbreviation for fanatic. Check the dictionary, Colin, fanatic is a person with an extreme and often unquestioning enthusiasm, devotion, or zeal for something, such as a religion, political stance, or cause. That's right, a Man City supporter. Or a true supporter of any other club for that matter.

Anyway, that's off my chest for the time being, so what actually happened in those first 10 minutes of my City football journey. Well, not a lot, actually.

Five weeks later, of course, the teams met again at Wembley in the FA Cup Final where we made up for the disappointment of losing to Newcastle the previous season by beating the Midlanders 3-1.

The match was made famous for Bert Trautmann, in the City goal, breaking his neck but playing on.

Joe Hayes, who scored in this League encounter, also got on the scoresheet in the Final, along with Bobby Johnstone and Jack Dyson.

CROWD CONTROL? In 1955-56, City's attendances varied from a high of 63,925 for the fixture against Blackpool on September 24 1955 to a low of 13,998 for Charlton's visit to Maine Road on March 21 1956. The Charlton attendance was the lowest for any City game – home or away that campaign. Highest away crowd was 60,956 at Old Trafford on New Year's Eve, where we ushered in the New Year by losing 2-1.

LONG-LIVED LONG THROW SPECIALIST Gordon Astall, who featured in the Birmingham team, was England's oldest living international at the time of his death in October 2020. He was 93. Astall played twice for England in 1956, against Finland (scoring on his debut) and West Germany. Astall, who was on the losing side in that year's FA Cup Final against City, was one of the earliest proponents of the long throw-in. Stoke City's Rory Delap, father of our current youngster Liam, was one of a number of players who followed in Astall's footsteps.

Chapter 2

BEATEN BY THE BUTCHER BOYS

City 1 Burnley 2
Maine Road
First Division
Monday 2 May 1960
Attendance: 65,981

City: Trautmann, Branagan, Sear, Barnes, Ewing, Oakes, Colbridge, Barlow, Hayes, Law, Hannah. [**Hayes**]
Manager: Les McDowall

Burnley: Blacklaw, Angus, Elder, Adamson, Cummings, Miller, Meredith, McIlroy, Pointer, Robson, Pilkington. [**Pilkington**, **Meredith**]

POSTMAN Pat and Fireman Sam are cult figures, certainly among the kids. But how about Bob the Butcher?

Well, if you're a Burnley fan of a certain age then Bob the Butcher – aka Bob Lord – would be your hero in the same way that Roman Abramovich is revered by Chelsea fans and Sheikh Mansour is adored by City supporters.

For Bob the Butcher* was the man who bankrolled Burnley to such an extent that this footballing outpost beat the big boys at their own game to win the First Division title in 1959-60.

And they climaxed what was probably the greatest season in their history on a May night at Maine Road.

I remember walking up to the turnstiles to take up my position at the back of the Platt Lane end and seeing quite a lot of Wolves fans who were stationed outside, hoping that City could win and hand them the title.

In those days, of course, there was no internet and no TV coverage of a game that would nowadays have had a huge build-up on Sky Sports.

The Wolves fans and thousands of others who were locked out with the gates closed had to listen to the crowd noises in an attempt to work out what was going on inside the ground, but Stan Cullis, the Wolves manager, made full use of his complimentary ticket.

Maine Road was heaving with the biggest attendance of the season – 65,891 – easily eclipsing the previous best of 58,300 for the derby game against Manchester United the previous September.

It was an uncomfortable evening in more ways than one. With it being a night fixture, a lot of the crowd turned up in the last 20 minutes or so before kick-off with the result that those people behind me were pushing forward to get better positions to see the drama unfold.

I spent a lot of the time just struggling to get back up the terraces after a surge had sent large sections of the crowd around me tumbling downwards.

I'm not sure I actually saw Burnley take the lead after only four minutes such was the scramble to keep my footing in the early going, but the noise from the Burnley fans told the story: Pilkington had scored after an uncharacteristic misjudgement by Trautmann. I read later that the Burnley player's effort was more of a cross than a shot, but whatever it was Burnley were ahead.

Things settled down in the crowd and on the pitch and what I did see of the action was a close-fought game despite the gap between the two teams, with City well down the table, but clear of the relegation places by the time this final game of the season was played.

And it was no surprise when Hayes equalised. A free-kick was floated over the Burnley defence and although Denis Law failed to control it, the ball came out to Hayes who gave Blacklaw no chance.

But on 31 minutes, Burnley were back in front and top of the table again when Trevor Meredith, standing in for the Clarets' England international John Connelly, sent the visiting fans into ecstasy with a shot that Trautmann couldn't reach.

The Burnley winner came after Ewing had given away a free-kick and after the ball had bobbed around the City area on the bone-hard, late-season surface, Branagan sliced a clearance straight to the diminutive Burnley winger.

ALL WHITE ON THE NIGHT At one point, the crowd began to chant "White ball! White ball! White ball!" over and over again. The flight of the ball was difficult to follow under the Maine Road lights and eventually the referee acceded to the crowd's request!

BOWING OUT City full back Ken Branagan made his final appearance for City in this match. He played 197 times for the Blues before being transferred to Oldham Athletic, his only other club in a 16-year career, where he featured in 176 matches. Branagan was twelfth man for City in the 1955 Cup Final against Newcastle, but under FA rules of the day, didn't qualify for a medal – an omission that was put right many years later after a campaign by the club and its former players' association.

When Branagan retired he opened a newsagents in Cadishead, Salford and had a spell as a coach at Oldham before leaving that role to run a betting shop in Golborne, Greater Manchester.

NOT THEIR FIRST TITLE Burnley's victory brought them their second title. They had topped the First Division table at the end of the 1920-21 season and it was City who finished runners-up, five points in arrears. After losing their first three games, the Clarets went on a 30-game unbeaten run, which was eventually snapped by City who beat them 3-0 at Hyde Road.

Burnley's unbeaten record was to stand for 80 years until Arsenal's 2003-04 side went through the whole 38-game League season unbeaten, winning 26 and drawing 12.

CAN THEY WIN IT AGAIN? It's unlikely that Burnley will be title winners again in the current era, but under manager Sean Dyche, whose gravelly-voiced instructions were clearly heard across empty stadia during the lockdown season, they are also unlikely to go down either. However, their recent record against the Blues is not good to say the least. Since beating us 1-0 in March 2015, the Blues have recorded 12 Premier League wins and a draw, including a record-breaking four consecutive 5-0 home wins. Can we play you every week?

*With apologies to Bob the Builder, who didn't quite fit in with the theme.

Chapter 3

A LAW UNTO HIMSELF

Luton Town 2 City 6
(abandoned after 69 minutes – waterlogged pitch)
Kenilworth Road
FA Cup Fourth Round
Saturday, 28 January 1961
Attendance: 23,727

Luton Town: Standen, McNally, Bramwell, Pacey, Groves, McGuffie, Noake, Ashworth, Turner, Brown, Fleming. [**Ashworth** 2]

City: Trautmann, Leivers, Betts, Barnes, Plenderleith, Shawcross, Barlow, Law, Hannah, Hayes, Baker. [**Law** 6]

Manager: Les McDowall

IT'S the pub question to end all pub questions: Who scored seven goals in an FA Cup tie and ended up on the losing side?

And yes, it was a City player.

And yes, Denis Law is the answer.

It all happened in the fourth round after the Blues were drawn away to Luton Town.

On paper, it was a tough tie, City were mid-table in Division One, while the home team were in the Second Division, having been relegated in bottom place the season before.

And defeat for the Blues wouldn't have registered too high on the Richter Scale of Cup shocks. We were heading for mid-table mediocrity, thirteenth place, while the Hatters ended up in exactly the same position in the second tier.

Arriving at Kenilworth Road, it was wet, wet, wet – and the rain didn't relent for a single second of the game.

It had been tipping it down over this part of Bedfordshire for several days and there were doubts whether the game would go ahead.

One journalist, previewing the clashed, described the pitch as "a beach with the tide just out, then deep mud, then a shallow lake".

But referee Ken Tuck decided the game could go ahead.

At least I felt at home on the open terrace behind the goal – we had brought the Manchester weather with us, we joked.

But the joke – and the wet stuff – was very much on us as Luton stormed into a two-goal lead with both goals scored by Southport-born ex-Everton centre-forward Alec Ashworth.

But gradually City got a grip, albeit a rather slippery one, on the game, and no one revelled in the atrocious conditions better than Law.

The City fans in the 23,727 crowd – and most of the locals – were open-mouthed as Law netted again – and again and again.

He had scored both to level things up at 2-2 and kept on scoring as we, literally, slid into a 6-2 lead.

I vividly remember Jimmy Meadows, our head coach at the time, walking behind the goal after attending to an injured player – presumably with the 'magic sponge' – being asked by City fans with the score 4-2 in our favour: 'What's going on Jimmy?"

He just smiled and shrugged his shoulders. We didn't know either!

Meadows, of course, will always be remembered for the serious injury he suffered in the 17th minute of the Blues' FA Cup Final against Newcastle in 1955 in the days when substitutes weren't allowed. Ten-men City lost 3-1 and Meadows was forced to retire from the playing side to join the coaching staff at Maine Road.

Soon after Meadows' on-field intervention, Law was hammering another two goals to send us into what we believed was an unassailable 6-2 lead and a place in the fifth round.

But it was noticeable that the Luton players were losing their footing more and more – often right in front of the referee.

Eventually, Tuck took notice, and with the rain showing no sign of abating, the ref led the players from the field; Luton's lads getting off the pitch as quickly as possible, while City's were more than a little reluctant.

There were just 21 minutes left, plus any added time, but the players never came back and eventually it was announced that the game had been abandoned.

It was an 'I was there, but I still don't believe it' moment.

All that was left was to traipse back into Luton town centre and get back on the train for Manchester.

By then, of course, even the rain had had enough!

Never mind, eh. We'll go through whenever the game is re-scheduled. Won't we?

It was re-arranged for the following Wednesday, and Typical City lost 3-1 with Law scoring the only goal!

So, seven goals in a single tie, and the Scot still finished on the losing side...

And Law actually felt that the game four days later shouldn't have gone ahead.

"The funny thing," he said, "was when we went for the replay [sic] on the Wednesday the pitch was in a worse state than it ever was on Saturday!"

DID YOU KNOW? Modern-day VAR, that scourge of the game that was supposed to make everything better, would probably have ruled out one of Law's six-pack?

One of his goal-bound efforts may well have come off a Luton defender, but without the benefit of action replays or the dreaded VAR, it was credited to Law anyway. Who would have wanted to deny him getting all six?

However, in a *Dundee Evening Telegraph* article printed in May 2017, reader Andy Walker suggested that Law "only" scored 5.

Walker, responding to a recent query about Law's six-goal haul, said: "Not one to court controversy, I have to say that Denis Law NEVER scored six goals against Luton Town while playing for Manchester City in the FA Cup.

"He actually scored just five – and was 'credited' with another.

"In a goalmouth melee on a pitch that resembled a tattie field, four players scrambled for the ball. Denis, running in, collided with the keeper. The ball spilled out, but Denis went for it again, only this time he had to get past a Luton defender.

"Law leapt and, as he did so, the Luton goalie tipped the ball sideways towards his team-mate Foines, who stretched to connect with the ball. It hit the Luton man on the back of the calf and rolled over the line, just as Denis landed.

"Now, who got the last touch of the ball?

"In the absence then of TV replays, the press attending couldn't make it out, and a radio broadcaster likewise.

Andy concluded: "However, it is a great story. Denis has been quite open about it, too, and he has suggested himself the defender might have scored an own goal."

Only problem here is that 'Foines' mentioned in the above article wasn't on the Luton team sheet for the game – and subs weren't allowed in the competition for another six years! Never let the facts get in the way of a good yarn, they say.

DID YOU KNOW? Had his goals counted, Law would have been the 20th century's top FA Cup goalscorer. Instead, the honour goes to former Liverpool striker Ian Rush. Law finished the century with 41 official FA Cup goals compared to Rush's 44.

DID YOU KNOW? Law signed for City from Huddersfield for £53,000 in March 1960 when his signing on fee was just £20!

His wages were £20 a week during the season and £17 in the summer. This was at a time when Jimmy Hill was trying to get Professional Footballers' Association members a better deal.

So, it was no wonder that John Charles – the best in Britain at the time – had already left Leeds to join Juventus for £70 a week plus bonuses as well as an apartment and car.

Ten months after Law's double hat-trick, the Football League offered an extra £10 a week on the maximum wage, but Hill argued for the government conciliation specialist to arbitrate the dispute.

The League folded and a truce was hammered out at the Ministry of Labour abolishing the £20 ceiling in the face of a threat of strike action.

The clubs tried – unsuccessfully – to renege on the agreement almost before the ink was dry on the deal, but the players won out in the end.

Fast forward to today's astronomical signing-on fees, agents' fees and stratospheric salaries in the Premier League.

Law was born well before his time...

Chapter 4

CAN WE PLAY YOU EVERY WEEK?

City 8 Scunthorpe United 1
Maine Road
Second Division
Boxing Day, Thursday, 26 December, 1963
Attendance: 26,365

City: Dowd, Leivers, Sear, Kennedy, Wood, Oakes, Murray, Young, Gray, Wagstaffe, Kevan. [**Murray 3, Gray 3, Kevan 2**]

Manager: George Poyser

Scunthorpe United: Jones, Hemstead, Brownswood, Gibson, Horstead, Gannon, Crawford, Hodgson, Kirkman, Lawther, Wilson. [**Lawther**]

I AM fairly sure that fans asking, "Can we play you every week?" wasn't part of the footballing lexicon back in the 1960s.

But it would have been a really good question after this one-sided thrashing.

And two days later, City went to the Old Show Ground and hammered The Iron 4-2.

We might not have been able to play Scunthorpe every week, but when we did, we played them off the park as can be seen from our six-wins-in-six games record against them with 30 goals scored and only seven conceded.

The "first leg" of this holiday double-header constituted City's biggest-ever Christmas win – and it came hard on the heels of a 6-1 success over Rotherham United.

The Blues were in eighth place prior to kick-off with Scunthorpe struggling 11 places below them.

And the visitors defended so well in the first half that they were only a goal down at the interval.

Then the floodgates opened and 25 minutes after the break we were 7-0 to the good.

Matt Gray scored a hat-trick inside 12 minutes, Jimmy Murray also grabbed three and Derek Kevan two – so only three scorers all told.

Lawther managed to get on the scoresheet for Scunthorpe to prevent his side from recording the heaviest defeat in their history.

That also came during the festive season, on Christmas Day 1952, when Scunthorpe handed out the presents in the form of an 8-0 loss against Carlisle.

I think that Scunny legend Jack Brownsword, who played in a record 791 first team games for the Lincolnshire club, missed a penalty in this particular defeat although I can't remember what the score was at the time.

Brownsword's failure was a major surprise as the left-back was reckoned to be a faultless penalty taker, scoring a remarkable 52 of his 53 career goals from the spot.

But he faltered that day and I remember a Scunthorpe supporter standing in front of me – away fans were allowed in the Kippax then I believe – holding his head in his hands in disbelief. As if conceding eight goals wasn't enough. It might well have been Brownsword's first-ever penalty miss.

However, this win and the big win over Rotherham didn't trigger a run to the title or a cup triumph. Far from it, in our next five games we suffered three League defeats and were knocked out of both the FA Cup and League Cup.

DID YOU KNOW? Jack Brownsword, who missed the Scunthorpe penalty, was rumoured at one time to have turned down "a lucrative move" to City. Brownsword stayed put and spent 18 seasons with the Lincolnshire team, making his final appearance at the age of 41. He also played a major part in former Blues manager Kevin Keegan moving from Scunthorpe to Liverpool, having recommended the player to Anfield manager Bill Shankly.

ANOTHER CHRISTMAS GIFT To complete a great Boxing Day, Manchester United were beaten 6-1 at Burnley.

CRICKET CONNECTION England great Ian Botham once played for Scunthorpe before deciding to concentrate on cricket. Good decision.

CITY CONNECTION Peter Beagrie and Alan Kirkman were two Blues who also played for The Iron. Beagrie, now a TV pundit, famously dropped down three divisions to join Scunthorpe when Bradford City were relegated from the Premier League at the end of the 2000-01 season. He joined City from Everton for £1.1million and made 52 appearances for the club.

NEXT VISIT Scunthorpe, by then in the Fourth Division, made their next visit to Maine Road in September 1974 when they lost 6-0 in a League Cup tie under the management of Ron Bradley (no me, neither). Colin Bell scored a hat-trick for the Blues.

DOUBLING UP City played – and beat – Scunthorpe twice in the 2009-10 season, winning their FA Cup and League encounters against The Iron. The FA Cup match was the first time in Scunthorpe's history that the club had appeared live on terrestrial television.

PHEW! Scunthorpe avoided relegation from Division Two at the end of the 2020-21 season by three points despite no wins from their last ten games. They finished in 22nd place.

They have never played at elite level, either in the old First Division or the new Premier League. Their visit to Maine Road on Boxing Day was during their six-season tenure in Division Two between 1958 and 1964. However, Scunthorpe have played three seasons in the Championship (2007-08, 2009-10 and 2010-11).

GOAL GLUT Boxing Day 1963 saw 66 goals scored in the First Division. In addition to United's loss to Burnley (see above), Fulham beat Ipswich 10-1 at home (only to lose the reverse fixture two days later), while Blackburn notched a remarkable 8-2 win at West Ham.

Chapter 5

LOWEST OF THE LOW

City 1 Swindon Town 2
Maine Road
Second Division
Saturday, 16 January 1965
Attendance: 8,015

City: Dowd, Bacuzzi, Sear, Kennedy, Gratrix, Oakes, Pardoe, Murray, Kevan, Ogden, Connor. [**Oakes**]

Manager: George Poyser

Swindon Hicks, Dawson, Trollope, Morgan, McPherson, Atherton, Shergold, Hunt, Summerbee, Brown, Rogers. [**Brown**, **Summerbee**]

THE DISHEARTENING defeat by Swindon will always be remembered as one of the bleakest moments in the club's history.

With a lowest-ever home League crowd of just 8,015 in attendance at Maine Road that miserable afternoon, the few who were there will never forget just how grim the future looked.

But perhaps what is less well known was that this was the first time that a young centre-forward by the name of Mike Summerbee came to the club's attention.

The 22-year-old, christened "Buzzer" by teammates and fans, would blossom as a winger and become one of City's 'Holy Trinity' of Bell, Lee and Summerbee.

It was later that day that Swindon's *Football Pink* would mention City's possible pursuit of the talented youngster.

Under the headline, 'City interest in Summerbee', the two-paragraph story that ran alongside the report of Swindon's success and was bylined *RCC*, informed readers: "*Reports circulating in Manchester today indicate that the City* (sic) *are interested in Michael Summerbee – as a winger. It is indicated in the local paper that he had been watched and that his form was duly noted this afternoon, though there was no comment from the City* (sic iterum)."

The two things to duly note, to borrow the paper's phrase, are that there was a measure of surprise that the Blues wanted Summerbee, who had been playing at No.9, as a winger, and that they twice referred to the Blues as 'the City' as though they were some sort of City of London hedge fund.

But the speculation was bang on target and Summerbee duly became one of Joe Mercer's most inspired signing in the following July, duly plying his trade on the wing to great effect and adulation.

At the time, however, the buzz was all about the crowd – or the lack of it.

There were some extenuating circumstances. There was rain throughout the morning – now there's a surprise in Manchester – and the referee only allowed the game to go ahead after a pre-match inspection. As I remember it, there was a good deal of rain over the 90 minutes as well.

City were in fair form at the time and although Swindon weren't the most attractive of visitors – Summerbee excepted – it was still a bit of surprise that the match-up produced the club's lowest League attendance at Maine Road for a first team fixture.

In fact, there were so few in the ground that many of those in the cavernous Kippax Street Stand were able to sit throughout. Perhaps a forerunner of all-seater stadiums...

The match itself mirrored the poor turn-out with Swindon grabbing both points with a goal in each half. Summerbee had a hand in the first, scored by Dennis Brown, and added the second himself before

Alan Oakes got City's with a long-range effort.

Swindon keeper Tony Hicks was the busier of the two men between the sticks but despite a lot of late pressure, Swindon hung on for the points.

It was a bit of a "park the bus" effort even though that phrase wouldn't enter the football dictionary for many years.

As *RCC* put in in the aforementioned *Football Pink*, "With Hicks doing some fine work in goal, Swindon's defence-in-depth policy, topped up by sharp attacks worked out well at Maine Road".

So, a bit of a backs-to-the-wall, hit them on the break kind of effort. Sound familiar?

In fifth place after this defeat, the Blues eventually dropped down to finish eleventh. But the following season with Mercer and Malcolm Allison starting their partnership, they were to win the Second Division title and return to the top tier, with the aforementioned Summerbee starting in every match, the only player in the side to do so.

HOW MANY WERE REALLY AT THE GAME? A long time after this low-point crowd-wise, City became a major power in the English game and those seeking tickets for big games, especially Wembley finals or semi-finals, would always say 'I was at the Swindon game you know...' On that basis it was almost certainly a full house at Maine Road on that wet and wintry day in January!

DID YOU KNOW? Preston-born Summerbee was signed from Swindon for a bargain £35,000. He had made more than 200 appearances for the Wiltshire club, netting 38 times.

LIKE FATHER, LIKE SON Well, almost. Summerbee's son Nicky also played for Swindon before joining City, but never quite hit the heights his old man did.

PRACTICAL JOKER Summerbee Senior had a reputation for being a practical joker and also had a fiery temper – a trait described by teammate Francis Lee as "retaliating first".

UP AND DOWN CROWDS In the days before Sky invented the

Premier League, crowds would vary greatly from week to week unlike now when most top-tier grounds are at least 90 per cent full every week for League games at least. One of the biggest swings in numbers came at Maine Road in 1934 with only 13,908 watching the Blues beat Sheffield United 4-1 when a week earlier, admittedly in an FA Cup sixth round game, City had attracted a massive 84,569 to see them defeat Stoke City.

GONE SHOPPING The lowest recorded Premiership attendance was the scarcely believable total of 3,039 who turned up for Wimbledon's clash against Everton on 26 January 1993 – and that was decades before the era of social distancing. As one Everton fan is alleged to have said: "I got off the train and asked where the Wimbledon ground was. I was told 'follow the crowd', so I did – and ended up in Asda!"

HOW LOW CAN YOU GO? Some reports suggest that the lowest-ever Football League attendance was 13 – yes, 13 – at Old Trafford on 7 May 1921. In truth, they were the only paying customers who watched Stockport County against Leicester City in a Division Two game on that day. However, in mitigation, about 10,000 of the fans who had watched Manchester United's game against Derby County on the same ground earlier that same day stayed behind to watch Stockport, whose ground was closed at the time.

WAS THIS OUR LOWEST CROWD? Accurate attendance records only survive from the 1925-26 season and so it is not clear if the 8,000-crowd estimated for the Maine Road game against Sheffield United in February 1924 was actually lower than the 8,015 for this game against Swindon. We'll never know.

LOWEST OF THE LOW Almost 34 years later, in December 1998, only 3,007 bothered to turn up at Maine Road for an Auto Windscreens Shield North section match against Mansfield. The fans who stayed away didn't miss much; the Blues lost 2-1. To further rub in the ignominy, the next night, United had a full house at Old Trafford for their European Cup clash with Bayern Munich, en route to winning the competition.

Chapter 6

BUBBLY BELL SEALS PROMOTION

Rotherham United 0 City 1
Millmoor
Second Division
Wednesday 4 May 1966
Attendance: 11,376

Rotherham United: Jones, Wilcockson, Clish, Casper, Haselden, Tiler, Lyons, Chappell, Galley, Chambers, Pring.

City: Dowd, Kennedy, Horne, Pardoe, Heslop, Oakes, Summerbee, Bell, Young, Crossan, Connor. [**Bell**]

Manager: Joe Mercer

COLIN BELL claimed it was the first time he'd had a glass of bubbly.

He was never one for lavish celebrations on or off the pitch, but there was an excuse as this was the night City clinched promotion to the First Division under the new management axis of Joe Mercer and Malcolm Allison.

And it was the start of something really special in the club's history, an unprecedented run of success that included a League title, an FA Cup, a League Cup and a European crown.

Bell told author Ian Cheeseman who collaborated with the player for his *Colin Bell Reluctant Hero* book: "That was the first day I had tasted champagne. Malcolm had probably been carrying it around for the previous two games ready for when promotion came."

Knowing what we know now about Big Mal, it's pretty unlikely he had been lugging around a bottle of champers for a couple of hours let alone a couple of games.

Allison always lived life to full and though he probably didn't sprinkle the fizzy stuff on his morning cornflakes, he would never let a bottle go unopened for any length of time.

Bell certainly earned his 'glass half full' moment as he headed home the only goal of the game that sent City back to the First Division.

Victory left the Blues four points clear of second-placed Huddersfield Town and third-placed Coventry who each had only one game left, while Southampton in fourth had three games still to play.

Two games later and the Maine Road side were in an unassailable position at the head of the table.

Bell told Cheeseman: "I don't remember much about the game, although I know that by half-time my ankle was very swollen. They strapped my ankle on the outside of the boot. If I'd taken the boot off, I probably wouldn't have got it back on again. I played like that throughout the second half. It was during that period, playing down the hill, that I scored the vital goal to give us a 1-0 win and secure our place in the First Division. I don't think I've been back to Rotherham since."

Like Bell, I don't remember much about the game either, apart from the fact that the view wasn't all that great. All that mattered was Bell heading home right in front of the fans.

RABBIT HUTCH Bell says the Millmoor changing rooms were "fairly basic and almost totally constructed from wood. You could shake hands with the person opposite you because it was so narrow, unlike the big square rooms in most grounds".

AMEN TO THAT: The Rotherham programme noted: "A city like Manchester can support two First Division sides and, until this season, so much of the glory has laid on one side in recent years. It is nice to see, and read of, the success of 'coach-minded' management members like Joe Mercer and Malcolm Allison who have worked so hard for the game wherever it has taken them."

SEVEN-UP City had it much easier in 2019, beating the Millers 7-0 in the FA Cup third round at the Etihad in front of a 52,708 crowd that included 6,000 who had crossed the border from Yorkshire. As Paul Davis put it in the *Rotherham Advertiser*: "For 12 minutes, 6,000-plus Rotherham United fans dared to dream. Then Manchester City took the lead and there was no way back for the Millers."

NO HISTORY? Rotherham United came into being in 1925 when Rotherham County and Rotherham Town merged. They started off wearing yellow and black, but changed to red and white around 1930, which seems a shame. Under their various guises they played at Millmoor for 101 years before moving to the New York Stadium in 2012. Rotherham actually featured in the inaugural League Cup Final in 1961 against Aston Villa, winning the first leg 2-0 at home before losing the away leg 3-0 with Villa's winner being scored in extra time. Villa, ironically, were managed by none other than Joe Mercer. The competition got off to a difficult start with top-tier clubs Tottenham, Sheffield Wednesday, Wolves, Arsenal and West Brom not even bothering to enter. The League Cup is now, I think, sponsored by City.

PERSONAL NOTE I was at Spotland in 1962 when Rochdale hosted Norwich in the first leg of the final of the following year's League Cup, losing 3-0. Rochdale were beaten 1-0 in the away leg for a 4-0 aggregate loss.

Chapter 7

THE DAY WE ICED SPURS

City 4 Tottenham Hotspur 1
First Division
Maine Road
Saturday, 9 December 1967
Attendance: 35,792

City: Mulhearn, Book, Pardoe, Oakes, Heslop, Doyle, Bell, Coleman, Lee, Young, Summerbee. [**Bell, Summerbee, Coleman, Young**]

Manager: Joe Mercer

Tottenham Hotspur: Jennings, Kinnear, Knowles, Mackay, Mullery, Hoy, Jones, Saul, Greaves, Venables, Gilzean. [**Greaves**]

EVERY City fan – young and old – knows or should know about the legendary 'Ballet on Ice' that played out on this bitterly cold winter's day at Maine Road.

But until I began researching this book, I was unaware of one of the major reasons behind the Blues extraordinary display.

Apparently, a lot of the credit should go to City's wily skipper Tony Book, who remembered a tip he had been given by a former coach during his long-distant youth team days.

With a heavy snowfall on the morning of the match causing the referee to make two inspections before allowing the game to go ahead, Book told his players to take off the top layer of leather from their studs.

It would let the nails show through giving the players much better grip on the treacherous surface.

Even allowing for the fact that no ref would have passed this pitch fit for play nowadays (see Chapter 47), Book's ploy would have fallen foul of the normal boots and studs' inspection carried out these days.

But players in the 60s were obviously made of sterner stuff – at least City players were, and while Spurs "didn't fancy it" as the modern vernacular might put it, the Blues just got on with it.

"Just getting on with it" is palpably unfair. They actually relished the task at hand, while Spurs manager Bill Nicholson, one of the game's greats, admitted: "It was incredible. One team wanted to play and the other didn't. It was one of the most remarkable things I've ever seen. While we slipped and slithered around, they played as though the conditions didn't exist."

It was a truly outstanding performance that made a lasting impression and will almost certainly never be equalled at the top level – thanks to a combination of undersoil heating, over-fussy referees and pampered players.

The conditions *were* unplayable – and so were we! If the City team had been Olympic figure skaters, all of them would have got top marks for artistic impression. Gold medals all round.

I was lucky enough to be there, but if you don't believe just how good City were, check out the YouTube clips. You'll be amazed.

The Blues even had to fight back from going a goal down when poacher supreme Jimmy Greaves pounced after a Terry Venables free kick had been pushed out by Mulhearn.

With the snow sweeping across the terraces, City, now getting more attuned to the atrocious surface, equalised with a goal from Bell, but couldn't get in front, as their attacking play richly deserved, before the interval.

Young, gliding over the surface, hit the bar with Jennings, who performed miracles throughout to keep the score down, well beaten.

By the second half the falling snow had turned to sleet, but a Summerbee header on 50 minutes, from a Young cross, warmed the crowd as City took a 2-1 lead.

On 64 minutes, Lee hit the post and Coleman followed up to make it 3-1.

Then Young finally got on the scoresheet to make it 4-1 in the 75th minute and that's how it stayed despite City hitting both posts in the same movement late in the game.

ONLY MATCH OF THE SEASON The game was named as the 'Match of the Season' by *Match of the Day* and, surprisingly considering today's wall-to-wall coverage, it was the only time the TV cameras paid a visit to Maine Road.

NOT WRONG Before kick-off, legendary BBC commentator Kenneth Wolstenholme called City "the most exciting team in England".

BOTTOMS UP City keeper Ken Mulhearn wore tracksuit bottoms, while Jennings looked in discomfort on the frozen turf, but pluckily played on. He was easily Spurs best performer over the 90 minutes.

HAPPY ENDING City who retained third place behind Liverpool after this fixture went on to pip Manchester United to the title on the last day of the season (see Chapter 8).

WHAT THEY SAID Tony Book: "That was the day I knew we were genuine title contenders. It was a fantastic performance, the best in my time at City." **Colin Bell:** "Pat Jennings was in goal for Tottenham and what a keeper he was. You'd shake hands with him and realise his hands were three times as big as yours. He saved everything early on." **Glyn Pardoe:** "There was a suggestion Tottenham wanted the game postponed but that wasn't the case in our dressing room. We just wanted to get on and make the best of it."

TURNING UP THE HEAT It wasn't until the 1970s that undersoil became popular although Everton were well ahead of the curve, being the first team to install it, in 1958. However, it wasn't used at Maine Road until the 1982-83 season. In 1971 Leicester tried to keep their Filbert Street pitch playable in winter weather by covering the ground with a giant tent, called a polysphere, which was kept afloat by giant blowers. The players were even able to train underneath the tent. It cost £5,000 but proved an expensive flop. Back in the 1920s, Tottenham used haybales to try to stave off frost, but it didn't work and only succeeded in making the pitch look like a farmyard.

Chapter 8

TITLE WON IN A SEVEN-GOAL THRILLER

Newcastle United 3 City 4
St James' Park
First Division
Saturday 11 May 1968
Attendance: 46,492

Newcastle United: McFaul; Craig, Clark; Moncur, McNamee, Iley; Sinclair, Scott, Davies, B Robson, T Robson. [**Robson**, **Sinclair**, **McNamee**]

City: Mulhearn; Book, Pardoe; Doyle, Heslop, Oakes; Lee, Bell, Summerbee, Young, Coleman. [**Summerbee**, **Young** 2, **Lee**]

Manager: Joe Mercer

HER Majesty the Queen didn't officially open the M62 motorway until October 1971, so the journey to Newcastle was a lot longer than it is today.

Much longer, actually, as it was almost bumper to bumper along the M1, with cars of all shapes and sizes, some roadworthy, others not so, jamming the road towards St James' Park.

We even spotted one with the nameplate 'Hotpoint Supermatic' although none of my fellow passengers could determine what model of what car it really was!

It was slow going and we even got chatting to a horsebox driver alongside us. He told he was taking a horse up to Gosforth Park for a race that afternoon.

"He's called Rock Signal," he told us. "Remember the name.". We didn't.

In all the excitement of getting to our biggest game for many years, we all forgot it. Only the next day when I checked the racing results in the Sunday paper did I realise it had won!

It mattered not. The only win we were interested in was a City one. They needed to beat Newcastle to clinch their first title in 31 long, hard years.

The game was tense, emotional, end-to-end, and above all, it was a classic.

The word 'classic' is overused in sport in general and in football in particular, but this had everything. It was a true classic in every sense of the word – and I was drained at the end of the 90 minutes.

The First Division title – and a place in the European Cup for the first time in City's history – was at stake.

And there was no complicated mathematics needed to work out the task that lay ahead: if City won there was nothing that United could do about it in their home match against Sunderland. Shades of that Aguerooo moment here when Sunderland, once again, were United's opponents on that fateful day in 2012. But that, of course, was an age away into the future.

At St James' Park, back in '68, City almost went a goal down very early on when Newcastle's Jim Scott hit the bar with Mulhearn beaten.

But soon afterwards, in the 14th minute, Summerbee put us ahead, latching onto a pass from Doyle. We were going crazy – for about 60 seconds! That was all it took for Bryan Robson to make it 1-1 with a superb effort after Heslop "went missing" way up field after a failed tackle.

But it was "Nellie" – Neil Young – with a shot that matched Robson's for brilliance, who restored our lead in the 32nd minute.

Again, the lead didn't last long – all of five minutes – in this topsy-turvy contest as Jackie Sinclair restored parity for the home side from long range. It was 2-2 and we were still in the first half!

We'd found out that Sunderland were beating United at half time, but were just focused on the two points and they edged a little closer when after great work by Bell we went in front yet again in the 49th minute. Bell's shot was cleared off the line and Young stepped in to belt it home. 3-2 ahead.

And even better was to come when Lee swept one home after an inch-perfect pass from Bell in the 63rd minute. 4-2. Fans all around were chanting 'Champions'.

We were almost there. Or were we?

In typical City fashion, McNamee pulled one back for the Magpies with four minutes plus stoppage time left on the clock.

I have no idea how many minutes were added to the 90, but it seemed like an eternity until that final whistle sounded and we were acclaimed as title winners.

It had been a long haul – more than three decades plus 90 minutes that just seemed like 30 years!

As the respected Manchester Evening News journalist Eric Todd put it: "Thirty-one years have passed since City finished at the top of the tree, and 21 since the late Frank Swift assured me that City were a grand club but one inclined towards erratic behaviour. In the succeeding years, City have experienced relegation and promotion, and visits to Wembley in two successive seasons. They have wasted many thousands of pounds on new players, they have unearthed others from nowhere, so to say, and made them little short of great.

"In turn they have been visited by irresponsibility and outright inspiration. They have been brilliant and they have been quite dreadful. They have been lauded to the skies, and they have had their office windows smashed by disgruntled supporters. They were frequently as Lazarus at the rich man's gate. And nobody need inquire who in this context was the rich man. City spent a great deal of time, money and effort trying to catch, let alone keep up with, their neighbours along the way.

"It took a long time for City to see the light, and it must be a matter for speculation when that specific moment arrived. Or how. The establishment of the alliance in the summer of 1965 of Messrs Mercer and Allison? The unwavering faith of Mr AV Alexander, their chairman, who, like his father did before him, has given more than fifty years' service to City? The reorganisation of the board? The signings of such players as Mulhearn, Bell, Summerbee, Coleman, Lee, Heslop, Kennedy and Book, who did not enter League football until he was 28? The rapid development of Doyle, Pardoe, Oakes and Young, and one or two more from whom the best is yet to come? A combination or permutation of these factors has earned its just reward."

TERRYFYING PROPHECY? 'Just watch us terrify Europe' was the *Daily Mail*'s Monday headline, quoting Allison, who said: "Too many of the foreign coaches are cowards." Big Mal sort of got it right; just under two years later, the Blues won the European Cup Winners' Cup in Vienna (see Chapter 10).

PRAISE INDEED Legendary Liverpool manager Bill Shankly phoned Mercer to tell him: "It was the hardest ever championship to win. You had to beat 12 of the best teams the League has had in all the years I've been in football."

DOYLE DELIGHT I don't remember seeing it in all the pandemonium of taking a 2-1 lead, but looking at some of the footage, you can see Doyle lifting up the referee in delight after City had regained the lead! He might have been sent off for his "assault" these days!

DID YOU KNOW? Grainy footage on mancity.com and on YouTube underlines just how many City fans made the trip – and they were on all four sides of the ground, unlike today's segregated supporters' area. Estimates at the time put the figure of Blues in the crowd that day at around 20,000 – and I wouldn't disagree.

DID YOU KNOW? Bell played his first game for England, against Sweden at Wembley, just 11 days after City's title-clinching victory.

UNITED'S FAULT? Segregation didn't come in until after the 1973-

74 season when Manchester United were relegated to the Second Division and some of their fans caused mayhem up and down the country and in the same season, a Blackpool fan was stabbed to death at Bloomfield Road during a Second Division match. Fans were kept apart and a number of clubs erected fences at their grounds.

Unsurprisingly, the controversial Chelsea chairman Ken Bates went one better than a plain and simple fence to keep fans apart. He erected an electric fence at Stamford Bridge in the 1984-85 season, but was prevented from switching it on by the Greater London Council (GLC) prior to the London derby against Spurs in April. He appealed the GLC's decision, but lost.

Chapter 9

ALL'S WELL THAT ENDS WELL!

City 1 Leicester City 0
Wembley Stadium
FA Cup Final
Saturday 26 April 1969
Attendance: 100,000

City: Dowd, Book, Pardoe, Doyle, Booth, Oakes, Summerbee, Bell, Lee, Young, Coleman. [**Young**]

Manager: Joe Mercer

Leicester City: Shilton, Rodrigues, Nish, Roberts, Woollett, Cross, Fern, Gibson, Lochhead, Clarke, Glover (Manley).

RIGHT place, wrong time. How many times have you heard that expression? How about, wrong place, right time? Well, that was me.

I'd managed to buy a ticket at the last minute. Honestly, can't remember from whom. Could have been a tout; could have been a friend. No idea.

But naïve me, didn't check whether it was in the *right* part of the ground.

It wasn't. I was stuck slap, bang in the middle of the Leicester fans behind one of the goals. That's what I mean, wrong place, right time.

It was a slightly unnerving experience, but I suppose City blue and

Leicester City blue aren't too far apart, so no one really bothered me and I didn't really bother anyone either.

And it was only at the end when the City players went up the steps to the Royal Box to receive the Cup and the Foxes fans had drifted away as they tend to do on these occasions that I realised that there were about 50 Blues who had made the same "mistake" as I had.

Still, we were able to properly give vent to our feelings as skipper Tony Book, voted Player of the Year a few days earlier, collected the trophy from Princess Anne.

As reigning Division One champions, City were big favourites against a Leicester side which been battling most of the season to avoid relegation; a battle they were to lose.

And they lost this one too. But they didn't go down without a fight and at the end only Neil Young's goal separated the two sides.

Young's match-winner came in the 23rd minute and was set up by Summerbee who found him unmarked on the edge of the Foxes' box.

Nellie, as he was affectionately known to the fans, arrowed a perfect shot into the top corner, giving future England keeper Peter Shilton, scrambling to get across his line, no chance.

Young was one of the unsung heroes of a City side best known for its superstars Bell, Lee and Summerbee, but he often did the business – as he did on this afternoon at Wembley.

However, he retained the knack of not looking as if he was trying for most of his career, often coming off at half time on a mud-spattered pitch without a mark on his shorts! He was also known as a player who never fancied heading the ball.

No one could fault him this day though.

Before Young's clincher, Lee and Summerbee had combined to set up Tony Coleman with a real opportunity to put the Blues into an early lead, but he blasted the ball well over.

Lee had robbed a Leicester player in his usual all-action style and set Buzzer off down the byline, the former Swindon man outwitting Wood and doing wonders to keep the ball in play before slotting it back to Coleman.

At the other end, Allan Clarke almost sniffed out a chance for Leicester as he ran across the City backline before firing in a shot that had Harry Dowd at full stretch.

There were other chances for Leicester too with a Len Glover shot being kicked off the line with Dowd stranded.

But City withstood these threats and there were also several close calls for the Leicester goal, among them a Colin Bell free-kick.

The second half was a lot quieter than the first, but City always seemed to be in control and ran out worthy, if narrow, winners.

COLEMAN'S SAUCE On being introduced to Princess Anne, representing the Royal family at her first-ever Cup Final, Tony Coleman bowed politely and told her: "Pleased to meet you ma'am, give my love to your Mum and Dad!" That night The Queen sent Coleman a telegram thanking him for his good wishes.

DID YOU KNOW? Leicester were completing an unenviable "double", losing in the FA Cup Final and being relegated in the same season, something that hadn't happened since 1926, when, you've guessed, Manchester City "achieved" it!

KEEPING IN TOUCH Strange as it may seem, even in these days of ever more intrusive television, City manager Joe Mercer was interviewed on the touchline during the game, just after Young had given his side the lead. "I'm relieved now," said the Blues boss, wearing a trilby and overcoat, "Summerbee's playing magnificently and I think he made the goal." Mercer was alone as his lieutenant Malcolm Allison was serving a touchline ban and had been forced to sit in the stands.

ON BOTH CHANNELS The match was televised live on both BBC and ITV.

NOT TO BE SNIFFED AT Allan "Sniffer" Clarke, who had a great game for the Foxes and was named by journalists as Man of the Match, played only one season at Filbert Street. He had scored the winning goal in the semi-final success that took Leicester to Wembley – against West Brom, the team he had supported as a boy. Clarke was best known for his exploits at Leeds United and for England, making 19 international appearances. Clarke earned his nickname by sniffing out chances, which he did to good effect, scoring 285 times in 609 senior appearances in a career that also took in spells at Walsall, Fulham and Barnsley.

CABBAGE PATCH KIDS *The Times* anticipated the condition of the Wembley surface, telling their readers: "if — as it is said — it is in a good, lush state Manchester will be happy. If, on the other hand, it proves to be heavy, then it could suit Leicester the better." Joe Mercer wasn't amused when he saw conditions at first hand, describing the pitch as "a cabbage patch". And also in *The Times*, Geoffrey Green agreed. In his match report he said the Wembley turf was "a glutinous swamp".

DID YOU KNOW? According to the Pathe News commentator, the toss for ends before kick-off was done "with the new 50p piece", the world's first seven-sided coin and which replaced the ten-shilling note. However, the new coin wasn't officially introduced into circulation until seven months later, on October 14 that year.

Chapter 10

VIENNESE WALTZ

City 2 Gornik Zabrze 1
Prater Stadium, Vienna
European Cup-Winners' Cup Final
Wednesday 29 April 1970
Attendance: 10,000

City: Corrigan, Book, Pardoe, Doyle (Bowyer), Booth, Oakes, Heslop, Lee, Young Bell, Towers. [**Young, Lee**, pen]

Manager: Joe Mercer

Gornik: Kostka, Latocha, Ozlizlo, Gorgan, Forenski (Deja), Szoltysik, Wilczek, (Skowrone), Olek, Bana, Lubanski, Szaryniski. [**Ozlizlo**]

THE rain, picked out by the floodlights, slanted down incessantly from the black sky above the near-empty Prater Stadium.

It was more like Manchester than Vienna as the estimated 4,000 City fans in the sparse, crowd of around 10,000 ended up like drowned – but happy – rats as the Blues held on to win a European trophy for the first time in their history.

In the final ten minutes, with City resolutely defending their 2-1 advantage, I ended up only about 50 yards from the managerial duo of Joe Mercer and Malcolm Allison as they looked on with large, white towels covering their heads as they attempted to shelter from the terrible conditions.

But it had looked far from promising on the afternoon of the match after a friend and I had flown in for the game. The pair of us were strolling through one of the many parks close to the centre of the city when I was chased and threatened by a group of... City fans, who had mistaken us for Gornik supporters!

I had no idea why, but my friend didn't hang around to ask. He ran off in another direction, but thankfully, my Mancunian accent stopped this particular group of Blues from doing me any mischief.

With that narrow escape under my belt – and reunited with my "former" friend – it was all more or less plain sailing after that, especially in view of the torrential rain.

We were told that the game was being shown live in Austria, so there were few locals around, and no Gornik fans were allowed visas to let them travel from their homeland although I do remember seeing small knots of Polish fans dotted around.

Add the atrocious weather into the mix and you can see why the crowd was so sparse. Surprisingly, at the time the City contingent represented the largest number of English fans travelling for a European away game.

No one in the UK saw the game either. On the same evening, the infamous FA Cup Final replay between Chelsea and Leeds United was screened live by both BBC One and ITV with an audience of 28.5 million, the sixth most-watched programme in British TV history – a list headed at 32.3 million by England's World Cup Final win over West Germany in 1966.

But all of this mattered not a jot and those who did make it will never forget the occasion.

Summerbee missed out with an injury at the end of our 60-game season and with the Poles racking up 190 international caps between them, this was no pushover.

In truth, it was an entertaining spectacle despite the horrendous conditions and the eery atmosphere, with City's attack-minded team getting their reward early on when a great shot from Lee was pushed out by Gornik keeper Hubert Kostka, with Young following up to slam in the loose ball.

Lee and Young were both involved two minutes before half time when City doubled their lead. It happened when Young was clean through on goal, but was taken out by Kostka – "that foul on Neil was so bad the keeper would have been sent off twice these days," said Lee later.

As it was, Kostka escaped a dismissal, but could do nothing with Lee's fierce spot kick; a great way for Lee to celebrate his 26th birthday!

City splashed through the puddles to stay in control of the second half until a foul by Bell gave Gornik a free-kick from which their skipper Ozlizlo gave Corrigan no chance.

And there were still 32 minutes left. By then Doyle had gone off with an injured ankle to be replaced by Bowyer, who missed a big chance to put the game to bed, but City weathered the storm, on and off the pitch, to claim European honours.

Minutes after the final whistle, veteran skipper Tony Book was holding aloft City's fifth major trophy in three years following on from the First Division (1967-68), the Charity Shield and the FA Cup the following season and the League Cup in 1970.

Winning in Vienna meant the Blues were the first English side to complete a European and domestic cup double in the same season.

BIG BREAK The game gave commentator Barry Davies his big break at the BBC. He had only joined the channel about seven months earlier and here he was doing a European final.

In normal circumstances he wouldn't have been sent to cover a Euro final, but the FA Cup Final replay was being shown live that same night so Barry got the gig.

"I had only joined the BBC the previous September so in normal circumstances I would not have got a European final," he said.

"The Cup-Winners' Cup was a big deal at the time. Not as much as the European Cup of course, but even so it was considered a very important trophy. I was surprised the final was played the same night as the FA Cup Final replay."

The City game launched the likeable Davies on a stellar career in football broadcasting.

DID YOU KNOW? The Prater Stadium's capacity was expanded from 60,000 to 92,708 in 1956, but was lowered in 1965. Today it holds 50,000.

In the mid-1980s, way too late for City fans, the stadium was covered and fully seated!

It was renamed the Ernst Happel Stadium after Austria's iconic player and coach.

NAZI CONNECTION During the Nazi era, the Prater Stadium was used as a temporary prison for more than a thousand Polish-born Viennese Jews, most of whom were deported to the notorious Buchenwald death camp. A day after these prisoners were sent to their deaths, the stadium was back in use for a match.

DID YOU KNOW? On their way to the final City hammered Belgian side Lierse 8-0 on aggregate in the second round, winning 3-0 away and 5-0 at Maine Road.

Chapter 11

NOT SO SHREW-D

Shrewsbury Town 2 City 0
Gay Meadow
FA Cup Fourth round
Saturday 25 January 1979
Attendance: 14,215

City Corrigan, Donachie, Power, Owen, Watson, P Futcher, Channon, Deyna (Bell), Kidd, Hartford, Barnes.

Manager: Tony Book

Shrewsbury Wardle, King, Larkin, Turner, Griffin, Keay, Chapman, Atkins, Tong, Biggins, Maguire. [**Maguire, Chapman**]

THE Taming of the Shrews? More like the Shaming of the Blues.

But was it really such a shock or even a genuine giant killing in FA Cup terms?

City came into the game in dreadful form, having failed to win any of their previous 13 League matches, were down in fifteenth place in the First Division, and had struggled to get this far in the Cup, only managing to beat struggling Third Division side Rotherham United after a replay in the previous round.

And here they were up against a Shrewsbury side, riding high in second place in Rotherham's division, on an icy surface, in front of a sell-out crowd.

Malcolm Allison had returned to the coaching staff at Maine Road just three weeks earlier to join forces with manager Tony Book, so some much-needed improvement was anticipated.

But this place wasn't perhaps the place to expect it.

The name 'Gay Meadow' doesn't exactly strike fear into the hearts of opposition players and fans in the way that a trip to Anfield, Old Trafford, the Nou Camp or the Bernabeu might do, but nevertheless there was a slightly unnerving atmosphere as I took my place behind the goal.

Only five of the 16 scheduled cup-ties had survived typical January weather and the snow was piled high along the touchlines, which were also piled high with mainly young Shrewsbury supporters.

Ordinarily, it should have been a fairly straightforward task, but City with big name signings Dave Watson, Paul Futcher, Asa Hartford, Kaziu Deyna, Mick Channon and Brian Kidd in the side, adopted the wrong tactics for the conditions, trying to play an elaborate passing game when a more direct approach would have paid dividends.

And that route one approach proved the right way to go for the Shrews when in the ninth minute defender Jack Keay put Paul Maguire in the clear with a well-directed long ball.

Maguire's first attempt was saved by Corrigan, but the ball cannoned back into Maguire's path and the striker gleefully followed it into the net with Futcher trailing unavailingly in his wake.

The bone-hard, heavily sanded conditions simply didn't suit City's style, and Shrewsbury, managed by Graham Turner, took full advantage.

Corrigan was penalised for carrying the ball out of the area and managed to tip the resultant free-kick over the bar, but from the corner that ensued, Sammy Chapman climbed high above City's defence to send a glancing header into the net on 57 minutes. This time Maguire, with a perfectly flighted corner, was the provider.

There was plenty of time to get back, but frankly the Blues didn't look that dangerous and Shrewsbury held on for one of their most famous victories.

City went on to finish a very disappointing season down in fifteenth place, while Shrewsbury went on to win the Third Division title. In the next round they beat Aldershot after a replay, but then lost to top-tier Wolves in another replay in the quarter-finals.

IN THE TOP TEN This defeat made No.8 in the *Top Ten FA Cup Cock-ups* compiled for the *King of the Kippax* magazine by Alan Rainford. Top spot went to the 1-0 defeat by Fourth Division Halifax Town in January 1980.

ON THE MOVE: Shrewsbury were formed in 1876 with the present club coming into being in 1886. They were elected to Division Three North in 1950. The Shrews started off playing at the Racecourse Ground and subsequently moved to grounds at Ambler's Field, Sutton Lane and Copthorne Barracks before settling at Gay Meadow in 1910, where they remained for 97 years before relocating to the New Meadow.

ALL IS FORGIVEN City didn't hold it against the Shrews following this defeat. They opened the New Meadow in a friendly in 2007. This time the score was reversed with City winning 2-0. City boss Sven Goran-Eriksson fielded two teams, one in each half, and former Shrewsbury keeper Joe Hart played in the "second team", replacing Kasper Schmeichel, and was given a great reception by the home fans. Martin Petrov made his debut for the Blues and Geovanni was handed a first start on British soil. City's scorers were Bernardo Corradi and Paul Dickov.

HOW ARE YOU MANAGING? Malcolm Allison had two spells as manager at City. He was in charge from October 1971 to March 1973 when his 78 games brought him a win percentage of 41.03 and then again from July 1979 (six months after this defeat at Shrewsbury) to October 1980 when his win ratio from 60 games dropped to 25 per cent. To give some sort of comparison, Guardiola's win percentage is an astonishing 74 per cent from the 293 games he has been in charge of at the time of writing. Interestingly, the Blues have been managed by a committee for two separate spells, the first of which brought them a 100 per cent record of two games two wins between July 1912 and September 1912. The next time they tried it, between April 1965 and May 1965, it wasn't a success with the committee clocking up only one win in five for a 20 per cent strike rate.

WORKING THE CORACLE Fred Davies and his coracle was an enduring legend at Gay Meadow. Fred – not to be confused with a Shrews manager of the same name in charge between 1993 and 1997 – was a coracle maker who would retrieve any stray footballs from the Severn River that ran parallel to one side of the ground. With lower division centre-halves frequently lumping the ball out of harm's way, Fred was often a busy man but I can't remember him being in action on City's visit. The coracle is now on display in the National Football Museum in Manchester.

Chapter 12

THE FORGOTTEN FINAL

City 4 Chelsea 5
Wembley Stadium
Full Members' Cup Final
Sunday 23 March 1986
Attendance: 67,236

City: Nixon, Reid, Power, Redmond, McCarthy, Phillips, Lillis, May, Kinsey, McNab, Wilson. [**Kinsey, Lillis 2,** 1 pen**, Rougvie** og]

Manager: Billy McNeill

Chelsea: Francis, Wood, Rougvie, Bumstead, McLaughlin, Pates, Nevin, Spackman, Lee, Speedie, McAllister. [**Speedie 3, Lee 2**]

THE Full Members' Cup was the brainchild of Ken Bates, the man who bought Chelsea for £1 and sold the club, complete with an £80million debt, to Roman Abramovich for approximately £18million.

So, what could possibly go wrong?

It was devised in the wake of the Heysel tragedy when English clubs were banned from European competition after 39 fans died before the start of the European Cup Final between Liverpool and Juventus in Brussels.

It was laughed at by fans and pundits alike and only ran for seven years before it was quietly consigned to the dustbin marked 'Bad ideas' by the Football League.

But before it was laid to rest, Bates had the last laugh – as he almost always did – with Chelsea winning a decent enough game in the Final, while City gained some kudos simply by appearing in a final after a long spell in the wilderness.

Bates, who switched clubs more often than some people changed their cars, was chairman of the Football League when the Full Members' Cup was first mooted and was supported in his bid to launch the competition that nobody really wanted by Roy Noades, the then chairman of Crystal Palace.

Teams from the top two divisions were eligible and 21 of them took part in the inaugural campaign with only five of them from the First Division, the two Wembley finalists plus Coventry City, Oxford United and West Brom.

Meanwhile, four of the then Big Five (Liverpool, Everton, Tottenham and Manchester United) had qualified for Europe, but their passports had been "impounded" by UEFA, so they were shunted into the Screensport Super Cup, which proved an even bigger flop than the FMC.

And although the fans may not have taken the new competition to their hearts in the early stages, City, almost skint at the time, certainly embraced it.

The Blues won their group by beating Leeds United 6-1 with new signing Gordon Davies claiming a hat-trick and then knocking out Sheffield United thanks to a last-minute goal by Graham Baker.

After the group stages, City played a regional semi-final and a regional final to reach the Twin Towers.

They saw off Sunderland in a penalty shootout in the semi-final – goalkeeper Eric Nixon proving the hero – and then beat Hull over two legs in the Northern Final.

After losing the first leg 2-1, only 10,108 turned up at Maine Road to witness a dramatic 2-0 win as the 3-2 aggregate victory was secured in the last minute by Jim Melrose.

Incredibly, the "big game" at Wembley was played the day after City had battled back from 2-0 down to clinch a point in the Manchester derby, while Chelsea were beating Southampton 1-0 to stay in the title race (they eventually finished only sixth, 17 points behind champions Liverpool).

Even more incredibly, ten players from each side had been involved 24 hours earlier.

But the previous day's exertions didn't seem to bother the Blues in the opening stages as they were ahead inside ten minutes through Mark Lillis.

Amazingly, though, 1-0 up became 5-1 down after a David Speedie hat-trick (the first at Wembley since Geoff Hurst's in the 1966 World Cup Final win over West Germany) and a brace from stand-in striker Colin Lee put Chelsea firmly in the driving seat.

The Blues fought back, but it was too little too late as two goals from Lillis, one of them from the penalty spot, were sandwiched between a Doug Rougvie own goal, to give the scoreline a respectable look. Remarkably, our goals came in the 85th, 88th and 89th minutes.

Given another five minutes, we might actually have gone on to level the scores or even snatch an unlikely victory...

CASHING IN The Final grossed receipts of more than half a million – £508,000 to be exact.

CHANGING NAMES In subsequent seasons, the Full Members' Cup changed its name, probably in a vain attempt to fool the fans, and was known in later iterations as the Simod Cup (1987-89) and the Zenith Data Systems Cup (1989-92). Chelsea won it again in 1990, beating Middlesbrough 1-0 in the Final.

A NEW LOW Although it is generally accepted that City's attendance for the 1965 Second Division game against Swindon in 1965 was their lowest-ever for a League fixture (see Chapter 5), the Full Members' Cup set an unwanted record for the sparsest home crowd for a competitive City game when just 4,029 (diehard) fans turned out at Maine Road for the 6-1 thrashing of Leeds United. Coventry attracted only 1,066 for the visit of Millwall, while Fulham pulled in a paltry

2,022 versus Oxford. It was reported – although never corroborated – that just 12 Shrewsbury supporters travelled to the midweek game against Oxford, where the away contingent was outnumbered by the nine policeman and four stewards who were there to look after them.

QUICK TURNAROUND Commenting on the fact that both teams had to play the previous day, City winger Paul Simpson, who came on as a sub in both games, said: "It was ridiculous – Old Trafford on Saturday and Wembley on the Sunday was a hell of a weekend for us.

"I just remember getting straight on the bus from Old Trafford and going down to London.

"There was none of the massages or recovery you get after games today. They talk about eating in this 'golden hour' after the game. But we literally just got up the next day, and started preparing for the final."

Chapter 13

ALAN BALLS IT UP

City 2 Liverpool 2
Maine Road
Premier League
Sunday 5 May 1996
Attendance: 31,426

City: Immel, Brightwell, Curle, Symons, Brown, Clough (Kavelashvili), Kinkladze, Lomas, Summerbee, Quinn (Philips), Rosler [**Rosler** pen, **Symons**]

Manager: Alan Ball

Liverpool: James, Jones, Wright, Babb, Ruddock, McAteer, McManaman, Redknapp (Kennedy), Thomas, Fowler, Rush. [**Lomas** og, **Rush**]

GOING into the final day of the Premier League season, it was a minor miracle that City had any chance at all of surviving the dreaded drop.

The noose had been tightening around the collective necks of the team and manager Alan Ball almost from the first weeks of the campaign after Ball had overseen a terrible start to the 1995-96 season, taking just two points from a possible 33.

The hangman was walking towards the gallows...

Successive defeats at Anfield – 4-0 in the League Cup and 6-0 in the

League – added to the pressure on chairman Francis Lee to sack the manager.

And then football does what football does. It amazed everyone. City remembered how to win. Ball even landed a Manager of the Month award and new signing Georgi Kinkladze began to show his sublime skills although he was very much a one-man band.

But Ball's Blues were never a model of consistency even when they were playing much better than they had in the early part of the season and they were always in the relegation dogfight although successive wins over Sheffield Wednesday and Aston Villa had given them fresh hope.

All they required to stay up was to do better than either Coventry or Southampton on this final day of reckoning. The three clubs were all on 37 points with Bolton and QPR already doomed.

So, the equation was simple: better either Coventry's result against Leeds United or Saints' result against Wimbledon (still not mathematically safe but with a much healthier goal difference than ours) and we'd stay in the Prem.

It might have been a simple equation, but it wasn't a simple task on the field – and it got much, much harder when Steve Lomas scored at the wrong end to put Liverpool ahead after only six minutes.

I was at the end where Liverpool scored that opening goal and even though own goals aren't usually celebrated as much as "proper" goals, there was the distinct feeling that Liverpool were not all that bothered that they had gone in front.

In that era, players from teams in close proximity to each other were probably mates unlike today's footballers who live in a sort of social bubble, notwithstanding the Covid secure bubbles we've become used to in the last season or so.

Just before the interval the relegation battle went from Ben Nevis to Everest when Ian Rush made it to 2-0. Again, the Liverpool players didn't look too fussed. They were now 12-0 up in two and a half games between the sides.

But just when the trapdoor was about to open to send us into the

First Division, Kinkladze was brought down in the box and Rosler stepped up to score from the spot. Nineteen minutes left.

Then Symons levelled things at 2-2. Twelve minutes left.

Anything could happen.

And it did.

Somehow, the City bench heard that Wimbledon had scored against Southampton and that the Blues only needed to close the game out to maintain their Premier League status.

The players were told to hold onto the ball. Lomas, who skippered City that day, remembers: "Alan Ball called me over and said, 'We're [staying] up, kill this game off, just do whatever you can'."

But Quinn, who had been subbed after getting a knock and was watching the scores on a television in the tunnel, knew differently.

Now out of his kit and dressed, Quinn raced down the touchline to tell the players they needed a win not a draw.

And those fans in the stands with transistor radios stuck to their ears knew as well. They couldn't understand why City weren't on all-out attack trying for that winning goal.

It was all too late. City had only wasted a few minutes, some of which time was spent down by the corner flag, where the Liverpool players didn't seem all that keen to get the ball back, but the momentum had gone.

The trapdoor swung open.

There was no knee-jerk reaction from chairman Lee. He had stood by Ball throughout the season and the former England and Everton man was still in charge at the start of the following campaign.

But two defeats in the opening three games of 1996-97, the last of which was a 2-1 loss at Stoke City, sealed Ball's fate. His ongoing feud with the fans had not abated and he resigned to make way for Asa Hartford, who lasted eight games, Steve Coppell (six games) and Phil Neal (ten games) before Frank Clark brought some stability if not success with a 59-game tenure.

WHAT QUINN SAID LATER "I had gone off after about an hour and was watching it on TV, so I knew what the situation was. I had to run up the tunnel and get the message on that we needed another."

ROSLER ROW Uwe Rosler's relationship with Ball was stormy to say the least. After Ball had dropped him earlier in the season, the German international was asked by the media if there was an issue between him and the boss. He didn't hold back: "Yes, there is a massive problem between me and the manager. I'm not playing for him, I'm playing for this football club, my team-mates and our supporters – but not for Alan Ball."

DID YOU KNOW? Kinkladze was persuaded to stay on after this relegation, but left after our demotion two seasons later when we dropped into the third tier in 1997-98. Kinky will never be forgotten by City fans nor will his legendary goal against Southampton – one of the highlights of 1995-96 – when he beat five Saints defenders before scoring. Extraordinarily, that iconic moment failed to win Match of the Day's Goal of the Season competition, finishing second! It did, however, win MOTD's Goal of the Month for March.

Chapter 14

BETTER LATE THAN NEVER

Oh! Mister Porter, what shall I do?
I want to go to Birmingham
And they're taking me on to Crewe,
Music hall song made famous by Marie Lloyd

City 1 Wigan Athletic 0
Maine Road
Second Division Play-off Semi-final Second leg
Wednesday, 19 May 1999
Attendance: 31,305

City: Weaver, Crooks, Edghill, Vaughan, Horlock, Wiekens, Brown, Jeff Whitley, Dickov, Goater, Cooke. [**Goater**] Used subs: Taylor, Pollock.

Manager: Joe Royle

Wigan Carroll, Green, Sharp, McGibbon, Balmer, Porter, Liddell, Greenall, Lowe, Bradshaw, Barlow. Used subs: Jones, Lee, Kilford.

IT WAS the biggest game we had ever played in Division Two – and there I was sitting on a train in Euston Station en route to Manchester for the match. Only problem, there was no driver!

Something to do with "staff shortages" we were continually being told over the train's communication system.

'Euston, we have a problem', so to speak.

We were told we'd be on our way as soon as they could locate someone who had the requisite skills to switch on the ignition – or whatever train drivers do – and get us on our way.

The minutes ticking by seemed like hours until, finally, a substitute driver, who had probably been warming up trackside for a while, was recruited for the job.

And so, we were on our way. Many minutes late by now.

But there was another concern that I forgot to mention. As all trains to Manchester were booked at this time, I'd only managed to book a Liverpool-bound choo-choo, having been told categorically that there would be a connecting train to Manchester arriving at Crewe soon after we'd got there.

Alas, we must have hit a lot of red signals. Don't you always when you're late?

So many reds that by the time we steamed into the Midlands we were in among the colours.

Back in the days before mobile phones with the internet on them, there was no way of knowing whether my late, late arrival in Crewe would still allow me to collect a Manchester-bound conveyance to get me to the game on time.

It didn't.

I had to jump on one billed as 'all-stations to Manchester Piccadilly' that was guaranteed to get me into the city centre well after kick-off. I toyed with the idea of getting off before then and grabbing a cab, but stayed aboard for the full scenic journey, jumping into a taxi on arrival.

He did his best and even put the radio commentary on for me, but I was almost too nervous to listen by now. I thrust some notes into his hand and legged it into the ground.

I'd just reached the top of the steps to where my seat was and caught my first glimpse of the action when the ball went into the net. I had no idea which way we were kicking, but milliseconds later a tremendous roar ripped through the ground.

It was Shaun Goater wheeling away to be mobbed by his teammates. I sat down exhausted. I will always know how late I was getting in. Goater's goal came on 27 minutes.

After the 1-1 draw at Springfield Park, where we had gone behind after just 17 seconds following a terrible mix-up between Nicky Weaver and Gerard Wiekens, it was a marvellous position to be in. We had gradually turned the tie around and were in sight of those fabled Twin Towers.

I didn't know it at the time, of course, but Goater might have handled the ball in the course of making sure it ended up in the back of the net. He had his back to me at the time so I couldn't tell and there weren't the myriad camera angles offered nowadays by Sky and other broadcasters. So, who knows?

But in retrospect that was probably the last piece of luck we have had with handball, offside and VAR decisions in more than two decades since that incident.

The Bermudan would go on to become a Man City icon – and in the process improve dramatically over the ensuing years, particularly his first touch, which in those days often let him down.

But that's another story.

Now there just 18 minutes or so left to half time. I felt elated and disorientated in equal measure.

Prior to Goater's strike, I understand Wigan had a decent shout for a penalty after a clumsy challenge by Gerard Wiekens, one which was in the 'I've seen them given' category.

And we had several good chances as well, including a diving header from Paul Dickov, but his glory moment was to come a little later...

Wigan fought back like demons in the second period and six minutes from the end of normal time came close to grabbing an equaliser from a free-kick which was headed against the bar from close range with Nicky Weaver beaten; the keeper's glory moment would come later too...

I've never been a nail-biter; could never see the point, but I came close that night as Wigan pressed and pressed.

Every time a player in blue had the ball at his feet, he seemed determined to get rid of it like it was a hot potato he wanted no part of. Understandably, no one wanted to make a mistake that might rob us of a trip to Wembley for the first time in 14 years.

Joe Royle's team were the division's form team with only two defeats in their previous 22 games, but form very often counts for nothing in the white-hot heat of a one-off cup-tie, which is what this game had turned into for both sides.

But bar a few nerve-shredding moments, City held on to book their date with destiny at Wembley Stadium.

At the final whistle there was a great outpouring of relief as fans flooded onto the pitch to salute their heroes.

However, there was more work to be done, much more, before they could exit football's third tier.

YOU'VE GOT TO HAND IT TO HIM Goalscoring hero Shaun Goater claimed years later that the referee had asked him: "'*That wasn't handball, was it?*' He had given the goal and I couldn't believe he was asking me that question ten seconds later! As if I would have said 'Yes' anyway. The truth is the ball never touched any part of my arm...'"

DID YOU KNOW? Goater was released by Man United and revered by Man City. He was granted the freedom of Bermuda in 2000 and every year on June 21, Shaun Goater Day is celebrated on the island.

DID YOU KNOW? Nicky Weaver's clean sheet in this game was his 23rd in his first full season between the sticks for the Blues.

UNAVAILABLE Skipper Andy Morrison and Ian Bishop were forced to miss the game through injury.

DID YOU KNOW? Paul Dickov's equaliser in the first leg of this semi-final was the last competitive goal scored at Springfield Park before Wigan moved to the JJB Stadium. At its peak, Springfield Park held 40,000, but only 6,762 turned up for that first leg.

Chapter 15

THE GREAT ESCAPE

City 2 Gillingham 2
(after extra time; score at 90 mins 2-2) (City won 3-1 on penalties)
Wembley Stadium
Second Division Play-off Final
Sunday 30 May 1999
Attendance: 76,935

City: Weaver, Crooks (Taylor), Edghill, Wiekens, Morrison, (Vaughan), Horlock, Brown (Bishop), Whitley, Dickov, Goater, Cooke. [**Horlock, Dickov**]

Manager: Joe Royle

Gillingham: Bartram, Southall, Ashby, Smith, Butters, Pennock, Patterson (Hodge), Hessenthaler, Asaba (Carr), Galloway (Saunders), Taylor. [**Asaba, Taylor**]

I HAD a great view of the action, slap, bang in the middle of a row right behind the goal City were attacking in the second half.

And that was what saved me from missing one of the most dramatic finishes in the club's history.

As Gillingham's second goal powered past Nicky Weaver in the 86th minute, I decided, along with hundreds of other Blues, that it was time to get out of there as quickly as possible.

I looked left along the row and then right, but very few, if any, fans in this section were getting up to go. I reckoned I'd have to disturb too many people, so resigned myself to sitting through the excruciating final few minutes left on the clock.

Later, there were stories galore, some true, some apocryphal, about City fans finding out that we had actually won and made it back into the First Division while they were taking a toilet break at Toddington Services.

Many of them, listening in or watching at home, must have wrecked their radios or trashed their televisions.

But who could blame them? I would have joined them if I could and been well down Wembley Way before the final minute of normal time when Kevin Horlock fired in from outside the box.

The goal came after some good interplay by the Blues, but there was a touch of luck as Gillingham looked to have cleared the danger only for the ball to finds its way to Horlock who found the net in great style.

But with the 90 minutes all but over there was some hope at last.

And it was Dickov who sent the Blues fans wild – and the match into extra time with a strike that would prove to be a turning point, not only in the game, but for the club's future.

The assist was provided by Shaun Goater, so it was a case of one legend providing another with a goalscoring opportunity and the ex-Gunners ace made no mistake.

Earlier before all the late drama, Gillingham had gone ahead on 81 minutes after Carl Asaba had started and finished a sweeping move and they made it 2-0 five minutes later, with Asaba the provider this time and Bob Taylor the scorer.

Once City had equalised, the Kent side were out on their feet, but to their credit didn't collapse, as might have been expected after having victory snatched out of their hands.

And so, the game went into a penalty shootout.

Goalscoring hero Horlock, his adrenaline levels as high as possible, was first up, sending Bartram the wrong way. **City 1-0**.

Paul Smith was the first penalty taker for Gillingham, but Weaver saved his effort with his feet. **City 1-0**.

However, unlike Horlock, Dickov's pen struck the post and although he followed up by putting it in the net, it didn't count. City **1-0**.

Adrian Pennock was next up for the Gills – and again they miss the target altogether. **City 1-0.**

Terry Cooke steps into the firing line and gives Bartram no chance, burying the ball in the bottom corner. **City 2-0.**

Finally, Gillingham get on the shootout scoresheet when John Hodge holds his nerve and puts his spot kick into the top corner. **City 2-1.**

But Richard Edghill restores our two-goal advantage as his effort goes in off the underside of the crossbar. **City 3-1.**

Guy Butters has got to convert to keep his side in the game, but Weaver goes the right way and makes the most important save of his career. **City 3-1.**

Cue Weaver's never-to-be-forgotten crazy celebration as he wheels away in delight with the rest of the City team in his wake and the fans – well, those that didn't manage to escape – in ecstasy in the stands.

Joe Royle's men were back where they belong. Well, not quite, but they had avoided a second season in tier three.

IT MIGHT HAVE BEEN OVER MUCH EARLIER Six minutes before Asaba had put Gillingham in front, a pass from Cooke had found Goater at the back post, but the Bermudan's shot struck the base of the post and bounced clear.

DID YOU KNOW? Dickov's goal (after four minutes and nine seconds of added time) remains the latest goal ever scored prior to the final whistle in a match at the old Wembley Stadium.

YOU COULDN'T MAKE IT UP Gillingham goalkeeper Vince Bartram was voted Man of the Match with the announcement coming just before City's first goal was scored – and he was also best man at Paul Dickov's wedding. If the judges had waited a little longer, they would almost certainly have given the verdict to either Dickov or Weaver.

DID YOU KNOW? This was the Gills first appearance at Wembley, while it was City's thirteenth if you count the 1981 FA Cup Final replay against Spurs, which I'd rather not! A year later, Gillingham were back at Wembley and this time they were successful against Wigan Athletic, but once more the game went into extra time with Gillingham getting home 3-1 with two extra-time goals after the game was deadlocked at 1-1 in 90 minutes.

WHEN THEY WERE STILL TALKING TO EACH OTHER Oasis stars Liam and Noel Gallagher were among the City fans celebrating the Blues success – about ten years before they fell out for the final time.

THEY WEREN'T TALKING TO EACH EITHER Reports suggested that Gillingham's controversial chairman Paul Scally and manager Tony Pulis had fallen out and were hardly speaking to each other in the build-up to the game. Scully eventually sacked Pulis for "gross misconduct" and an acrimonious legal battle ensued, with Pulis settling out of court for £75,000.

SCALLY-WAG Scally had demanded a replay when he spotted match referee Mark Halsey having a drink with City fans in a nearby hotel after the game. The appeal was quickly rejected, but that wasn't the end of the Scally story. In 2005, he was found guilty by an FA commission of placing bets on his own team and fined £10,000. One of his bets was on the Gills to lose the Play-Off Final – a neat (illegal) way of Scally cushioning the blow of the Kent's side's defeat.

Chapter 16

SUITS YOU, SIR

City 3 Portsmouth 1
Maine Road
First Division
Sunday, 21 April 2002
Attendance: 34,657

City: Nash, Pearce, Dunne, Howey (Wiekens), Horlock, Jensen, Benarbia, Wright-Phillips, Tiatto (Berkovic), Goater (Macken), Huckerby.

Manager: Kevin Keegan

Portsmouth: Beasant, Buxton, Primus, Vincent, Wilson, Quashie, Prosinecki, Harper, Summerbell, Pitt, Vine. Subs: Tardif, Barrett, Miglioranzi, Cooper, Brady. Subs used: Cooper, Brady.

I TURNED up in a suit for this one. I know...

Well, I couldn't get a "proper" ticket so I booked hospitality. A few of my mates spotted me walking around the ground before kick-off and I had to face a barrage of not-unexpected "Did you get the loan/ probation/ job?" remarks along the way.

Maybe, I had unwittingly started the trend for football fans wearing fancy dress on the final day of the season. Maybe not, as it seems Hartlepool supporters began the craze about nine years later when they appeared as Oompa Loompas; in later years they became penguins, Smurfs, Bob Marley fans, Stormtroopers and Thunderbirds.

Whether I was ahead of the sartorial game or not didn't really concern me. All I was worried about was finding my seat at my allotted table in what was, to me, an alien part of the ground. Eventually I got there and even shared a few words with club ambassador Mike Summerbee, who many years later kindly penned the foreword for this tome.

I can't remember what he said – and I'm sure he can't remember what I said either – but suitably fed and watered, I sat down in a decent-enough seat quite close to one of the corner flags as the Blues wound down and said a fond farewell to the fans after a long season in which they had clinched their first title since 1968.

It meant a return to the Promised Land, better known as the Premier League, and they had done it in style too with this victory against Pompey taking them to 31 wins for the campaign.

There was a valedictory goal for The Goat – aka Shaun Goater – his 32nd of 2001-02.

And another cult hero, Paul Dickov, came back to say his goodbyes.

All that was lacking was a fitting finale for Stuart Pearce, who had scored 99 goals in 1,000-plus games coming into the fixture.

His big chance to make it a ton arrived four minutes into stoppage time when Linvoy Primus was judged to have handled the ball.

Pearce, who famously missed a spot-kick for England at Italia 90, took his time.

Portsmouth goalkeeper Dave Beasant even had a little chat with him, allegedly telling "Psycho" exactly which way he planned to dive.

After all, neither team had anything to play for. This was going to be easy. All he had to do was get it on target...

But Pearce got it all wrong, blasting the ball over the bar.

It took a little of the icing off the cake, but not much. Pearce was heading into retirement with his first-ever title-winning medal.

It certainly didn't stop Blues fans from celebrating long after the game was over as Pearce, Goater, Dickov and the others took their bows.

Steve Howey had put City ahead inside ten minutes, powering

home a header from a Pearce cross, and Huckerby had crashed one against the post, before Player of the Year Ali Bernarbia set up Goater to make it 2-0.

Pompey pulled a goal back when Prosinecki swung over a corner, Kevin Harper flicked the ball on and Courtney Pitt bundled the ball over the line at the near post.

But on 86 minutes, City's two-goal advantage was restored when Jensen's ball into the box was guided past Beasant by Macken.

Then came Pearce's penalty howler.

PEARCE PAYS THE PENALTY Pearce remained at City as a coach under Keegan before, in March 2005, he was appointed caretaker manager after Keegan left the club. He was made permanent manager after a good run of form. In the 2005-06 season, City started well, but fell away dramatically, losing nine of their last ten games and there was no improvement in the following campaign when the club flirted with relegation. Scoring goals was a major problem with only ten at home all season and none at all after New Year's Day. Fans made their feeling clear with some even tearing up their season tickets before games and Pearce failed to survive. He was sacked in May 2007.

FOWLER HOWLER AS EXPERIMENT GOES WRONG In May 2005 and with City needing a goal to beat Middlesbrough to book a place in the UEFA Cup, Pearce decided to move keeper David James up front for the final eight or nine minutes, leaving striker Jon Macken on the bench with sub keeper Nicky Weaver going in goal. But a late penalty howler by Robbie Fowler sealed their fate in a 1-1 draw. It was Weaver's Premier League debut for the club – a debut he won't forget. Weaver recalled later in his career: "When I look back, it was my girlfriend's first game and she said afterwards: 'Does that happen all the time?' and I said: 'You'll never see that for the rest of your life.'"

CUP FINAL WIN OVER POMPEY The most famous meeting between the two club was in the 1934 FA Cup Final, which City won 2-1 after going a goal behind. Freddie Tilson scored both our goals. When referee Stanley Rous blew the final whistle, 19-year-old City keeper Frank Swift fainted. It was that sort of day. Rous, later Sir Stanley, became one of football's greatest administrators. He was president of FIFA (1961-74) and secretary of the FA (1934-62).

Chapter 17

TYPICAL CITY

City 0 Southampton 1
Maine Road
First Division
Sunday 1 May 2003
Attendance: 34,957

City: Schmeichel, Dunne (Horlock), Sommeil, Distin, Jensen, Wright-Phillips, Barton (Belmadi), Foe, Benarbia, Goater (Fowler), Anelka.

Manager: Kevin Keegan

Southampton: Jones, Telfer, Lundekvam, Michael Svensson, Bridge, Baird, Oakley, Anders Svensson (Tessem), Prutton (Higginbotham), Ormerod (Fernandes), Beattie. [**Svensson**]

TYPICAL City. It's a label we have worn – often with pride – down the years.

And I suppose this was a typical example of 'Typical City'.

It's the last game to be played at Maine Road, our home for 80 years before the move to the City of Manchester Stadium.

There's nothing at stake with both teams mired in mid-table.

The ground is almost full – just 193 below capacity at the time – and there's a party atmosphere as we bid farewell to one of the most iconic venues in world football.

The living legend that is Shaun Goater is made captain for the day, while the other Shaun, Wright-Phillips, has dyed his hair blue for the occasion.

The sun is shining and the fans are in good heart, even those who have allegedly paid upwards of £250 for the privilege of saying goodbye to Moss Side's most famous landmark.

But nobody told Southampton they were the uninvited guests at a private party. You know, the one standing alone in the corner drinking as much as he or she can until the host or hostess tells them they've come to the wrong address.

Once the pre-match celebrations were over, a game of football broke out, and after a slow start, City began to dominate with Saints keeper Paul Jones making several good saves in a fairly one-way first-half, with Vivien-Foe, Wright-Phillips, Bernarbia and Anelka prominent.

But on 34 minutes, Saints' Michal Svensson scored what proved to be the only goal of the game and the last competitive goal ever scored at Maine Road.

It wasn't for lack of trying that City didn't grab an equaliser, but the occasion mattered more than the result and Southampton held on for victory.

GOAT TRIBUTE Shaun Goater was replaced by Robbie Fowler on the hour, going off to a well-deserved standing ovation.

FOE TRAGEDY Marc Vivien-Foe, who was on loan at City from Lyon, tragically died less than two months later playing for Cameroon against Colombia in the Confederations Cup semi-final at Lyon's Stade de Gerland. He was 28. Foe made 35 appearances in sky blue, scoring nine goals, the last of which was against Sunderland in a 3-0 win when he actually netted the last-ever City goal at Maine Road. City "retired" his No.23 shirt and there is a permanent tribute to him in the memorial garden at the Etihad.

LUCKY NUMBER City keeper Peter Schmeichel was making his final appearance, having played 648 club games and 129 internationals for his native Denmark for a total of 777. Peter played 292 times for

United. His son Kasper started his career with the Blues, making eight starts.

SORRY SAINT Southampton boss Gordon Strachan said: "I know we have spoilt their celebrations, but it's right they should be celebrating the last game at this stadium, it's been a magnificent place for them."

KEEGAN'S COMMENTS The City boss said: "The best thing about the club are the fans and it will be the same in the new stadium. We finished ninth so we have done okay. I think we have under-performed, but if you ask the fans, I think they would probably be quite pleased.

"We have lost eight games here – nine if you count the cup – and I have told the players it is not good enough for me or the supporters, who have been magnificent.

"Maybe it is my job and the board's job to raise expectations. We have got to get away from 'We will lose today because we are Man City'. That hurts me more than anything.

"This club has got a losing mentality – it is us that causes that, players and management – and we have got to put that right."

DOGGONE The match could have been billed as 'Goodbye Dog Kennel Lane' as that was the original name of the street on which the ground was built back in 1923.

MAINE FACTS Record attendance was 84,569 for City's FA Cup tie against Stoke. Highest City League crowd was 79,491 for the game against Arsenal the following year. Before its closure Maine Road was an all-seater stadium and the capacity had shrunk to 35,150.

Before City's departure from Maine Road there were proposals for either Stockport County or rugby union side Sale Sharks to make use of the stadium, but the plans came to nothing and the ground was bulldozed to make way for a housing development.

Original plans for Maine Road were for a 120,000-capacity stadium, but these were scaled down considerably. The land – a former brickworks – was purchased for £5,500.

After the Second World War, Manchester United shared the venue after Old Trafford suffered bomb damage. They paid City £5,000 per season plus a share of gate receipts, which was 10 per cent less tax, except for the derby match which was pegged at £25.

Gary James, who wrote *Manchester: A Football History*, said of the ground-sharing scenario: "It is forgotten to some extent. United's support definitely increased during that period. You had a situation where fans would go to Maine Road every week to watch both teams. City fans and players would always want United to win if they were in a cup final for example and vice versa. And the attitude from City fans was 'let's help United any way we can'."

United also used Maine Road to host three of their four home games in the 1965-57 European Cup as Old Trafford didn't have floodlights.

Maine Road was used for several scenes in the 1948 film *Cup-tie Honeymoon* and was also featured in the 2000 movie *There's Only One Jimmy Grimble* as well as the 2003 ITV drama *The Second Coming*, starring Christopher Eccleston.

The stadium has also hosted a number of concerts, including The Rolling Stones, Simple Minds, Queen, Fleetwood Mac, Pink Floyd, David Bowie, Bryan Adams, Jean Michel Jarre, Dire Straits, Guns N' Roses, David Cassidy, Prince and Oasis.

Chapter 18

ANOTHER EUROPEAN GLORY NIGHT

Total Network Solutions 0 City 2
(City won 7-0 on aggregate)
Millenium Stadium, Cardiff
UEFA Cup Qualifying Round second leg
Thursday 28 August 2003
Attendance: 10,123

Total Network Solutions: Williams; Naylor, Taylor, Aggrey, King; Ruscoe, Leah, Brabin, Davies (Becks), James Wood (Bridgewater); Jamie Wood (Wilde).

City: Weaver; Dunne, Wiekens, Bischoff; Flood, Negouai, Berkovic (Barton), Bosvelt (Whelan), Tiatto; Macken (Wright-Phillips), Huckerby. [**Negouai, Huckerby**]

Manager: Kevin Keegan

THE tie wasn't exactly on a knife-edge after a 5-0 home win in the first leg, but it's always worth the effort to see the Blues in action, especially in an away game in Europe – even if it was only across the border in Wales.

I was up against the clock on the journey there and unbeknownst to me at the time a speed camera had clocked me over the limit and a fine would wing its way to my home address just a couple of weeks later.

Putting the pedal to the metal hadn't saved that much time in the end though and my brother and I were forced to sort-of jog our way to the stadium, arriving as the teams were about to kick off.

It was an almost unreal sight that greeted us with the awe-inspiring Millenium Stadium (capacity about 74,000) playing host to only around 10,000 fans.

With City's following estimated at circa 8,000, it meant that the home side had sold only about 20 per cent of the tickets.

But we were just glad to be there to see City successfully get through their first European tie in 24 years.

TNS were a strange amalgam of the almost unpronounceable Llansantffraid-yn-Mechain (try putting that on the back of a shirt) in Powys, Wales and Oswestry in Shropshire, England.

Keegan put out a virtual second eleven, making nine changes from the first leg, leaving out star names like Distin, Sinclair, Anelka and Fowler from his starting line-up.

And with a squad that was nowhere near as strong as it has been in our more recent history, it showed as the Blues struggled to get into any sort of rhythm.

Two minutes before the break sloppy TNS defending at a corner from the right led to the ball falling kindly for Negouai and he glided it past Williams from eight yards.

But it wasn't until nine minutes from the end that Huckerby managed to put the game to bed with a close-range effort.

The result salvaged some pride for TNS, who fielded former Manchester United player Simon Davies, capped once by Wales, who showed in flashes why he was once a member of the same United youth team as Ryan Giggs.

DID YOU KNOW? The home leg was the first competitive game at the City of Manchester Stadium. Four days earlier City had beaten Barcelona 2-1 in a friendly to inaugurate the new ground. The stadium was built to house the 2002 Commonwealth Games and originally had a capacity of 41,000. The foundation stone was laid by the then Prime Minister Tony Blair three years earlier.

BOXED IN The Millenium Stadium features a retractable roof, but on a sultry evening it wasn't needed. It has a capacity of 74,500, but extra seats can be added for special events. Record attendance wasn't for either football or rugby, but for the Anthony Joshua-Carlos Takam world heavyweight title fight in October 2017 when 78,000 watched as Joshua retained his WBA, IBF and IBO crowns.

STRIP SHOW: TNS wore shirts that looked a little like Celtic's, but they didn't play like them in either leg.

DID YOU KNOW? TNS were the first club in the UK to be named solely after their sponsors from 1997 to 2006. In early 2006, TNS were taken over by British Telecom and the sponsorship deal lapsed. After a search for new names, including an attempt to sell the naming rights on eBay, the name "The New Saints" was agreed upon as appropriate to the history of both of the originally merged clubs: Llansantffraid was always known as "The Saints", while Oswestry had strong connections with Saint Oswald. They still carry TNS in their title, styling themselves, The New Saints (TNS).

REYNA DAY The day after the game, US international Claudio Reyna joined the club for £2.5 million after a move to Fulham for the same fee had collapsed. Reyna's time at City was dogged by injury and he made only 87 appearances in three and a half seasons before moving to Major League Soccer side New York Red Bulls. In the Big Apple, he spent almost as much time on the treatment table as he did on the pitch, finally calling time on his playing career in 2008.

RECORD BREAKERS More recently, City failed to overhaul The New Saints record of 27 wins in a row, set in 2016. The Cymru Premier outfit triumphed in 27 games in a row between August and December 2016, eclipsing the 26 straight wins by Dutch giants Ajax in 1971-72, to establish a new world record. City fell six short when Manchester United shocked them with a 2-0 success after winning 21 in a row in all competitions, something no English top-flight side had achieved before.

Chapter 19

BACK FROM THE DEAD

Tottenham Hotspur 3 City 4
White Hart Lane
FA Cup Fourth Round Replay
Wednesday, 4 February 2004
Attendance: 30,400

Tottenham Hotspur: Keller, Carr, King, Gardner, Ziege (Jackson), Davies, Richards, Brown, Dalmat, Keane, Postiga (Poyet) [**King, Keane, Ziege**]

City: Arason, Jihai, Dunne, Distin, Tarnat, Wright-Phillips, Barton, Bosvelt (Sibierski), Sinclair (McManaman), Anelka (Macken), Fowler. [**Distin, Bosvelt, Wright-Phillips, Macken**]

Manager: Kevin Keegan

THREE down and a man down at half time and with star striker Nicolas Anelka already off injured, City came back from the depths of sporting Hades to produce one of the greatest FA Cup comebacks of all time.

Having been held to a 1-1 draw at Maine Road, we didn't travel to north London with much confidence, especially as the Blues had notched just one win in their previous 18 games and were fielding a debutant keeper in Arni Arason, replacing the cup-tied David James.

We were expecting the worst – and we weren't disappointed as Ledley King, who had started the move, finished it by bending one into to the top left-hand corner to beat Arason. One behind after two minutes.

And it got even worse when Robbie Keane snapped up the second for Spurs eight minutes before Anelka limped off.

But that double whammy in what was proving a terrible first half wasn't the end of our woes as three minutes before half time, Barton was booked for a bad tackle on former City player Michael Brown, himself a player never known to shirk a confrontation. From the resultant free-kick, it was 3-0 for Spurs as Ziege slammed home their third.

You'd think that at least the 15-minute interval might give Kevin Keegan's side the chance to regroup. Not a bit of it.

As the players were walking off when the half ended, Barton, presumably still aggrieved about his yellow card – even though it was probably a borderline red – continued to make his feelings known to referee Rob Styles and was shown a second yellow, not that any of the City fans knew much about it at the time.

Singing 'We're going to the win the cup, so now you're going to believe us' throughout the break in typical gallows humour style, it was only when the teams came back onto the field that the more eagle-eyed among us noticed that we were a man light.

So, a combination of Everest and Kilimanjaro to climb in the 45 minutes remaining.

And then there was the slightest sniff of a fightback when Sylvain Distin headed home with precision and power from a set piece just three minutes after the restart.

But literally the tipping point of the game came soon after Distin's goal although none of us at the time thought it was anything more than a terrific double save by the City keeper.

It came from another fierce free kick by Ziege – the ball looked goalbound even from our vantage point at the other end of the ground. And yet, Arason, playing his first-ever game in the UK, managed to get his finger tips to the shot as it bounced off the bar and out to the waiting Gus Poyet.

Poyet drove it back towards goal, but Arason was alert to the danger and dived to grab the Uruguayan's shot to complete the second part of this particular rearguard effort. Without the keeper's heroics, it would have been 4-1 and almost certainly game over.

A massive piece of luck – and didn't we need a break – reduced the arrears to a single goal when a Paul Bosvelt's half-volley took a big deflection off Gardner, giving Kasey Keller no chance.

Unbelievably, Shaun Wright-Phillips made it 3-3, avoiding the offside trap, to lob the ball over the Spurs keeper after a great pass from Robbie Fowler.

If the dreaded VAR hadn't been more than 15 years away at this point, Wright-Phillips' goal would, I believe, have been disallowed.

But it wasn't. Cue wild celebrations in our corner of the Lane. We might even make it to extra time and a much-needed breather as our 10 men had played like 12 in the second half. There were 11 minutes left of normal time.

By the 90th minute, we looked to have done enough to take the tie into an extra half hour when, surely, Spurs' man advantage would kill us off.

It was then that John Macken, who in his five years at Maine Road had never been a fans' favourite, achieved legendary status this night, arrowing home a header from a pinpoint Michael Tarnat cross.

As Kevin McCarra in *The Guardian* wrote: "This may well be as great a comeback as English football has ever known."

Keegan went further: "It was the cup tie of my lifetime, really." At half time he had told his players: "We're playing for pride now and we're looking for a miracle."

It was a miracle all right.

SEVENTH HEAVEN City fans, gathered in one corner of White Hart Lane, had the fairly unique experience of seeing all seven goals scored at their end.

WHERE'S THE JOB CENTRE? City manager Kevin Keegan told

coach Derek Fazackerley as the team came out for the second half: "We're 3-0 down and a man down. Where's the nearest Job Centre?" He was probably only half joking!

UNKNOWN QUANTITY Reykjavik-born Arason, signed from Rosenborg, never made a single league appearance for City, leaving to join Valerenga (Norway) before having spells with Thana Royal Zulu (South Africa), Odd Grenland (Norway) and Lierse SK (Belgium). He played 71 times for Iceland. Before the Spurs game, Keegan had never seen Arason play.

SKY'S THE LIMIT The match was originally scheduled for live broadcast on Match of the Day, but BBC bosses felt there was more interest in Conference side Scarborough against Chelsea and the clash between Liverpool and Newcastle United. Ultimately, it went out live on Sky Sports, which didn't have too many City subscribers back in 2004.

Chapter 20

MAKING HIS MARK?

Streymur 0 City 2
Torsvollur Stadium, Torshavn
UEFA Cup First qualifying round first leg
Thursday 17 July 2008
Attendance: 5,400

Streymur: Torgard, Bo, Clementsen, Djurhuus, Foldgast (Davidsen), Bardur Olsen, Jacobsen (Brian Olsen), Hans Pauli Samuelsen (Eliasen), Hanssen, Arnbjorn Hansen, Niclassen.

City: Hart, Onuoha, Dunne, Richards, Ball, Ireland, Hamann (Fernandes), Johnson, Petrov, Jo (Evans), Vassell. [**Petrov, Hamann**]

Manager: Mark Hughes

THIS was the start of new era. Or was it?

There was a new manager, Mark Hughes, in the dugout and a new record signing, João Alves de Assis Silva, better known as Jo, leading the attack.

On this night in the Faroe Islands, the pair were a success, but neither of them will be fondly remembered by City fans.

Hughes failed to shake off the fact that he had played for the "other side", while Jo was a major flop at £19 million, scoring only six times in 41 appearances in all competitions.

Hughes was appointed manager just two days after Sven-Goran Eriksson had been fired and to be fair the new boss was part of an unprecedented period of player recruitment. Jo apart, the Welshman brought in big names like Vincent Kompany, Carlos Tevez, Nigel de Jong and Pablo Zabaleta, all of whom would do a great job for the club.

He was also in charge when "statement signing" Robhino joined for a new club record fee of £32.5 million although it was fairly clear at the time that Hughes knew as little about the purchase as most City fans.

On this warm night in the Faroes, Hughes was a winner against a side whose name sounded more like a single malt than a football team.

City had sneaked into the UEFA Cup via the Fair Play League, which was a bit of an embarrassment, but about 250 Blues fans turned up, eschewing the cricket season which was then in full swing.

Boosted by the away contingent, the home side, playing in Torshavn, pulled in an estimated 5,000, five times the capacity of their Vid Margair Stadium 15 miles away in Streymur.

Petrov grabbed a ninth-minute lead for the visitors after Johnson had stepped over a Vassell cross and Hamman made it 2-0 on 28 minutes with a powerful shot from outside the box.

Despite a shot count of 26-7 in their favour that was the end of the scoring as a far from fully-fit City side cruised through the game.

GONE FISHING Football fans will do anything to get to games – and City fans are no different. Well, perhaps they are. Prior to the match, a group of Blues supporters decided it would be a bit of a hoot if they drove to Aberdeen, boarded the overnight ferry to the Shetlands and then chartered a trawler to the Faroes on the morning of the match – as you do!

It was all going well until the weather turned nasty – as it tends to do in the Faroes – and the trawler couldn't make the trip.

By this time the local and international media had picked up on the story and the Faroes national airline, Atlantic Airways stepped in to allow the guys to complete the third and final leg of the trip.

Once there, Thomas Cook joined the publicity bonanza by finding them accommodation. And the story didn't end there; one of the fans was taken ill with appendicitis and had stay on the island for a week. He finally made it out of hospital in time for the trip back to Manchester, travelling with the Streymur team en route to the second leg aboard another Atlantic Airways flight.

SECOND LEG SWITCHED With the turf at Eastlands all cut up after a Bon Jovi concert, the return leg was switched to Barnsley's Oakwell ground. The game was a cross between a testimonial and a practice match with City winning 2-0 for a 4-0 aggregate success.

According to Neil Shaw in Dave Wallace's excellent *Us and Them*, "The sum total of the Barnsley efforts amounted to Wonderwall [over the loudspeaker system] and a couple of City flags draped over the seats near the corner flags in the opposite stand. A coachload of screaming Streymur schoolkids was hardly the missing ingredient as City kicked off to a backdrop of midsummer apathy."

Only 7,334, including some locals, bothered to turn up.

NO GO JO Brazilian Jo never really fitted in to Hughes' plans and was loaned out to Everton and Galatasaray. He played all over the world after that, finally rejoining his boyhood team, Corinthians, where at the time of writing, he is still playing aged 34. He represented his national side on 20 occasions.

He was a teammate of the legendary Ronaldinho at Atletico Mineiro, but they drifted apart after Jo hit rock-bottom form-wise during Brazil's 2014 World Cup campaign and turned to alcohol in a bid to forget his on-field troubles.

His football globetrotting saw him have spells in China, Japan, Russia and the UAE. He is now happy – and scoring regularly for Corinthians.

As he explained: "I'm aware that I made mistakes in the past. Before, I wasn't even capable of acknowledging that. But now I have found peace in my life." Good for him.

NICOLE IN CHARGE A female referee, Nicole Petignat, from

Switzerland, officiated.

MARKED MAN Hughes was manager at the time of the Abu Dhabi takeover in September 2008, but was replaced by Roberto Mancini 15 months later in December 2009.

Chapter 21

SCARF FACE

City 0 FC Midtjylland 1
Eastlands
UEFA Cup Second Qualifying Round First leg
Thursday 14 August 2008
Attendance: 17,200

City: Hart, Corluka, Richards, Dunne, Ben-Haim, Elano (Etuhu), Johnson, Gelson, Petrov, Caicedo (Bojinov), Sturridge.

Manager: Mark Hughes

FC Midtjylland: Heinze, Afriyie, Califf, Reid, Poulsen, Borring, Florescu, Thygesen, Olsen (Madsen), Salami (Flinta), Nworuh (Babantude). [**Olsen**]

FOOTBALL'S a game of two halves, but is it a game of scarves with two halves?

I'm not sure, but half-and-half scarves certainly engender their fair share of ridicule for those who dare to wear them.

I mean, how can you support both teams in a single game?

Maybe, you can if you're a 'football tourist' who reckons buying a two-tone scarf is probably better value than picking up a match day programme as a souvenir. I mean, you can't wear your overpriced programme on a cold night during a game in some lost corner of a foreign field.

And yet. I have a confession to make. Back in the day – and not really that long ago if you check out the dateline above – I purchased one of those reviled, not revered, half-and half scarves.

However, there were some mitigating circumstances. I had seen them on sale in a mixture of blue and red on my way into the ground. "Get your scarves, a fiver each" was how I remembered the sales pitch. I demurred.

On the way back, though, they'd been reduced – not in size but in price – to just three quid. A bargain, I thought, and it was becoming a little bit chilly. So why not.

And, to be fair, I did wear it quite often and as the years wore on, it was a reminder of possibly our worst home performance in a European competition, but not only that, it was a sort of 'I was there' statement, with a crowd – wrong word I think – just managing to creep over the 17,000-mark.

They were rewarded – and I think that's the wrong word too – with a fairly inept display which ended in a deserved defeat.

The only goal came in the 15th minute when Dunne was undone by a mistake and the Danes' Danny Olsen scored with a neat finish.

And that's how it stayed until German referee Babak Rafati mercifully brought proceedings to a close.

We did huff and puff a little but it all felt like a pre-season friendly and after a summer of woe off the field with the club's Thai owner Thaksin Shinawatra facing charges of corruption and abuse of power in his homeland, things were no better on the field.

Hughes had spoken out in the build-up to this game to deny claims that players were being sold without his knowledge because of the uncertainty surrounding Shinawatra.

Hughes had tried, unsuccessfully, to recruit Roque Santa Cruz from the Welshman's former club, Blackburn, and you could see why the manager wanted to add some firepower to a team that was missing three senior strikers in Jo, Benjani and Vassell.

Hughes drafted in youngsters Sturridge and Caicedo and in the few highlights, it was the former who struck the bar as City tried to hit back after Olsen's shock goal. But Sturridge could, and should, have done better.

Late on the normally reliable Petrov had a decent chance from a free-kick, but he hit the bar.

And after that we were all ready to hit the bar...

NO EXCUSES Mark Hughes said: "Perhaps we were a bit behind them in terms of sharpness and match fitness but that is no excuse.

"In the first half we had too many unforced errors. We needed to be more dynamic, show more personality, and to try to drive the play.

"We need to get up to speed before the weekend and hopefully this game will let us know where we are at and what we need to do."

NOT UP TO SPEED Unfortunately, the Blues didn't "get up to speed" in time for Aston Villa three days later, going down 4-2 at Villa Park in the opening Premier League match of the season.

WE BELIEVED Midtjylland's California-born defender Danny Califf said: "We had to believe that we could get a result. We had to match the effort and tonight it was enough.

"I think at the start of the match they didn't expect us to come out and take it to them with the energy and effort that we showed."

BY THE SKIN OF THEIR TEETH City scraped through in the second leg, levelling the tie on aggregate with an own goal in the final minute when a glancing header from Evans was deflected into the net by Califf to send the game into a penalty shoot-out. Joe Hart was the hero, saving two Midtjylland spot kicks before Corluka settled the tie.

QUARTER-FINALISTS Despite this less than auspicious start, City eventually topped their Group and went on to reach the quarter-finals of the competition, where they were beaten 4-3 on aggregate by Hamburg, losing the first leg away 3-1 before winning 2-1 in a pulsating return.

ON THE MONEY Six years after they bowed out to City, Midtjylland became known as 'Moneyball FC' when professional gambler Matthew Benham, a lifelong Brentford fan, became a majority shareholder of the Danish side. Benham used statistics and data analysis to bring in underrated players on the cheap, nurturing their talent and then selling them on for big profits. Two years before buying into Midtjylland, Benham bought Brentford.

The original Moneyball method was pioneered by Major League Baseball side Oakland Athletics in the 1990s to recruit undervalued players and helped them into the play-offs in 2002 and 2003 despite the fact that they had one of the lowest team salaries in the MLB.

Chapter 22

EDIN IN THE RIGHT DIRECTION

Notts County 1 City 1
Meadow Lane
Sunday, 30 January 2011
FA Cup Fourth Round
Attendance: 16,587

City: Hart, Richards (Kompany). Zabaleta (Kolarov), Boateng, Lescott, Milner, Barry, Viera, Toure, Dzeko, Jo (Silva). [**Dzeko**]

Manager: Roberto Mancini

Notts County: Nelson, Darby, Edwards, Pearce, Harley, Ravenhill, Bishop, Martin, Hughes, Gow (Hawley), Westcarr. [**Bishop**]

EDIN DZEKO's equalising goal against Queens Park Rangers, which brought the sides level in that scarcely believable 2012 title triumph, has never received the credit that it deserved.

Without the Bosnian heading home powerfully from a corner to make it 2-2 in stoppage time, Aguero would not have been afforded the opportunity to score that iconic winner.

Dzeko's goal almost certainly was instrumental in changing the course of history – certainly City's history.

Here, in a clash billed as the 'oldest club versus the richest club' Dzeko started on that long road towards, dare we say immortality, by scoring the first goal of his distinguished City career; an Etihad career in which he netted 50 times in 130 senior appearances.

On this day, it saved City's blushes against a team two divisions below them; in 2011, it started a decade of domestic dominance.

For me, too, it represented a first in a long "career" watching football – I was seated in the directors' box.

And it was all thanks to my wife's 'bestie', Sue, whose father Lou, was a former director of County and who was able to rustle up a ticket for me.

Truth be told, it felt a little alien – a bit like sitting with opposition fans at an away match when you can't get a ticket from the City allocation. I'd done that a few times (see Chapter 9) and have always tried to avoid the experience.

The half-time tea and biscuits made up for it a little. At that point, it was 0-0 so all to play for, but the pudding-like pitch, probably a consequence of Nottingham Rugby Club's temporary tenancy, wasn't ideal for our slick passing game.

County were proving much more direct and drew first blood when Neal Bishop headed home from an Alan Gow corner on 59 minutes. It was Bishop's first goal in almost a year.

Prior to Bishop's shock goal, the Blues had come close through Toure who produced a good save from County keeper Stuart Nelson and a left-foot effort from Barry brought out another good effort from the home custodian. Dzeko also headed over when he might have done better.

And Dzeko did better, much better, with the minutes ticking away and a giant-killing becoming more and more of a possibility.

It came in the 80th minute and it was as simple a goal as he ever scored in City's colours, steering the ball home from close range from a Richards cross. It was the striker's first repayment of the £27 million fee we paid Wolfsburg for his services.

Silva, who had replaced the almost invisible Jo, 20 minutes earlier, threaded an intricate crossfield pass to release Richards, who sprinted into space down the right flank for the umpteenth time and on this occasion the full-back's cross paid dividends as Dzeko applied the finishing touch with his left foot.

In those final 10 minutes or so, it seemed as though both sides had settled for a replay; County contemplating a healthy cash injection and City looking forward to playing on a much better surface.

MAN OF THE MATCH ITV voted for Notts County scorer Neal Bishop, who was booked after he celebrated with the home fans. The accolade should have gone to City's Richards, but plucky underdog goalscorer beats Premiership star every time as far as the TV companies are concerned.

MIND THE GAP The teams were 59 places apart in the pyramid at kick-off time.

BIG FAVOURITES The bookies made the Blues 5-2 ON favourites to win.

BOGEY TEAM? The last time the teams met, in 1991, a brilliant performance from Notts County keeper Steve Cherry earned the Magpies a 1-0 victory.

PULLING POWER City's visit attracted the first sell-out crowd to Meadow Lane in 16 years.

CITY'S REPLAY REPLY Almost three weeks later the sides met again at the Etihad and goals from Viera (2), Tevez, Dzeko and Richards added up to a 5-0 victory for the Blues. County put up a decent fight and the home side might have been a little flattered by the scoreline with three of their goals coming in the final seven minutes.

Chapter 23

CATCHING A COLD IN KIEV

Dynamo Kiev 2 City 0
Valeriy Lobanovskiy Stadium
Europa League
Thursday 10 March 2011
Attendance: 16,000

Dynamo Kiev: Shovkovskiy, Danilo Silva, Popov, Khacheridi, Vukojevic, Gusev, Eremenko, Yussuf, Shevchenko (Ninkovic), Yarmolenko, Milevskiy. [**Shevchenko, Gusev**]

City: Hart, Richards, Kompany, Zabaleta, Kolarov (Wright-Phillips), Lescott, Barry, Silva, Y Toure, Dzeko, Balotelli (Tevez).

Manager: Roberto Mancini

I NEARLY didn't survive the biting cold; the Blues didn't survive this first leg defeat, crashing out in the second leg despite winning 1-0 at Eastlands in the return.

The match reports I read on returning home suggested the temperature dropped to minus-four degrees, but believe me, it felt way, way lower than that, not helped by a City display that rarely threatened to heat up the night.

It remains, to this day, the coldest 90 minutes I have ever had to endure as a football fan; an evening I shared with 562 hardy Blues who made the trip.

Even wearing a thermal vest, thermal jumper, thermal jacket as well as two hats and a similar number of scarves, it was an uncomfortable watch. The 10pm kick-off wasn't a big help, either.

Not so, for the City supporter next to me. Well and truly hammered after drinking copious amounts of the cheap vodka that was freely available anywhere in the Ukrainian capital, he passed out at about the halfway stage. And he only recovered to ask me the score on waking just before the final whistle.

Add into the mix that he had turned up wearing shorts and I'm surprised he made it back home – if he ever did – and didn't end up in a local hospital suffering from hypothermia or frostbite in his nether regions.

I'm not sure whether City were suffering from the cold, but the locals seemed to take to the treacherous, frost-hardened surface far better than we did and it was no real surprise when former Chelsea and AC Milan striker Andriy Shevchenko put the hosts ahead after 25 minutes.

The 34-year-old, who was a thorn in City's side all night long, bundled the ball past Hart after latching onto a whipped-in cross from Yarmolenko.

But City, without top scorer Tevez who was on the bench, had two decent chances to take the lead before the home side scored. First, Silva split the Dynamo defence with an incisive through-ball but Richards couldn't get to it ahead of Kiev keeper Oleksandr Shovkovskiy.

And Silva was again in the thick of the action, just failing to get enough on a scuffed Zabaleta cross as Kiev escaped once more.

Dynamo had hammered Turkish side Besiktas 8-1 on aggregate in the last round and grew in confidence towards the end of the first half, with Shevchenko's cut-back causing all sorts of problems. Thankfully, it didn't fall to one of Shevchenko's team-mates.

Gusev then cut in from the left to drag a 20-yard shot wide, while Artem Milevskiy blazed over on the stroke of half-time.

Leading scorer and captain Tevez, who had been left out of the starting line-up by Mancini, started to make things happen when he came on to replace Balotelli and City almost drew level two minutes after his introduction when Barry laid the ball back to Toure whose 20-yard effort was touched wide by Shovkovskiy.

And although the Blues couldn't get what would have been a vital equaliser and away goal, they were at least keeping out the home side only to concede a second on 76 minutes when Gusev rifled home a flick-on from Artem Milevskiy to make life doubly difficult for the return leg.

LATE SHOW Balotelli was late coming out for the second half and looked in some discomfort, clutching his face, when he re-joined the action. It was later claimed that he was allergic to the local grass! It wasn't long before Tevez came on to replace the Italian, but Balotelli managed to get himself booked before returning to the sidelines.

BOSS'S BIG CALL Mancini had decided to start without top scorer Tevez and pair Dzeko with Balotelli up front.

HOME COMFORTS Dynamo Kiev were unbeaten at home since December 2009 coming into the match.

WHAT A SHOWER Despite the freezing conditions, the sprinklers were switched on after the final whistle, soaking the local TV reporters.

KNOCKED OUT City won the second leg 1-0 but went out of the competition 2-1 on aggregate in front of a crowd of 27,816. Kolarov scored our goal and Balotelli, who didn't enhance his reputation across the two ties, was sent off. He also missed a sitter from three yards and a header from a little further out, 12 yards. Strangely enough, 578 Dynamo Kiev fans made the trip – more than the number of City fans had managed to get out to Ukraine, although it's highly likely a good percentage of them were UK-based.

NO HANGOVER City didn't suffer too much of a hangover from this defeat, getting the better of Reading 1-0 at home in the FA Cup sixth round with a late goal from Richards just three days later. Victory set up a clash with Manchester United in a Wembley semi-final, where another 1-0 win put us into the final, where we triumphed against Stoke City, again by 1-0.

Chapter 24

YAYA'S DERBY DECIDER

City 1 Manchester United 0
Wembley Stadium
FA Cup Semi-final
Saturday, 16 April 2011
Attendance: 86,549

City: Hart, Kompany, Zabaleta, Kolarov, Lescott, Johnson (Wright-Phillips), Barry, Silva (Viera), De Jong, Y Toure, Balotelli [**Toure**]

Manager: Roberto Mancini

Manchester United: Van de Sar, Evra, Ferdinand, Vidic, O'Shea, (Fabio Da Silva), Park Ji-Sung, Carrick, Nani, Scholes, Valencia (Hernandez).

WAS this the tipping point – the same type of tipping point that Malcolm Gladwell writes about in his ground-breaking book of the same title, published 11 years earlier?

In his best-seller, Gladwell describes a tipping point as "the seemingly magical process by which some products, ideas and ways of behaving cross a threshold or 'tip' and take off".

So, was this the time when Abu Dhabi's 2008 takeover actually tipped over?

Of course, beating Manchester United is always a seminal moment, but this one felt different. It marked a changing of the guard; the old order had been shaken up by the new, better-funded, order.

The Noisy Neighbours had got even louder. They'd bought a new car; were having their drive done and the front garden landscaped...

Victory propelled the Blues to their first major Wembley Final for three long decades, thirty years of wasted opportunities and disappointing defeats.

And, believe me, it felt good. As good as it gets. Or as good as it got at the time. We had seen the future and we liked what we saw.

Before kick-off, though, our family gathering on one of the grassy slopes outside England's newish national stadium contained more black humour than cautious optimism.

Let's get the celebration in first was Plan A. We had no Plan B.

Early on our pessimism looked well founded. Dimitar Berbatov, in for the suspended Wayne Rooney, had two big opportunities inside a first half-hour that the Reds dominated, to give United the lead. Hart, later voted Man of the Match, spread himself well to save the first of these chances, while Berbatov missed badly with the second, laid on for him by Nani.

While United were without Rooney, City had to cope without the injured Tevez, but despite this big loss, the Blues gradually got their act together and Barry, Balotelli, Lescott and Kompany all had chances before Yaya Toure scored the game's only goal on 52 minutes.

Taking advantage of some hesitancy in the United defence and, finally, a bad mistake by Michael Carrick, Toure, showing power and poise and escaping a shirt-pulling attempt by Nemanja Vidic, managed to get the ball past Van der Sar and into the net.

City's cause was helped immeasurably over those inevitably nervous late minutes of the game when Paul Scholes saw red with 17 minutes of normal time left on the clock after a late and high lunge on Zabaleta. Jasper Carrot lookalike Mike Dean pointed straight to the dressing room.

SUPER MARIO? Mario Balotelli, one of four City players booked, was involved in an angry altercation with Rio Ferdinand at the final whistle after triumphantly brandishing his club badge in the direction of the United fans. Ferdinand, who had earlier in the day celebrated the birth of his third child, shouted a tirade of abuse at the Italian. Four or five United players joined in, pushing and pulling the shirt of the Italian, who just stood there smiling.

STEPPING OUT OF THE SHADOWS City fans celebrated wildly at the final whistle. Had they stepped out of the shadow of their cross-town rivals. Only time would tell...

FIRST WEMBLEY DERBY The game was the first Manchester derby hosted by Wembley Stadium.

POZ-ITIVE RESPONSE The City faithful turned their backs 'doing a Poznan' during and after the game. It had been adopted by Blues supporters following the club's Europa League group stage fixture against Polish side Lech Poznan in October 2010, and was also part of the home fans' repertoire at Celtic in Scotland, Deportivo Alaves in Spain and Western Sydney Wanderers in Australia. Cardiff City, Leicester City and Arsenal fans have all used it to mock City after beating the Blues. It is rarely seen now at the Etihad or at away games – after all, who wants to miss even a few moments of scintillating City action on the pitch?

FERGIE'S TOUCHLINE BAN Manchester United manager Alex Ferguson was forced to watch the match from the stands after being banned for a record five games and handed a £30,000 fine by the Football Association for his criticism of referees. The FA's hard-line stance came after Ferguson, who had originally been banned for three games, decided to fight the charge rather than accept that he had gone too far in his condemnation of Martin Atkinson after United's League defeat at Chelsea.

Chapter 25

TOURE DOES IT AGAIN

City 1 Stoke City 0
Wembley Stadium
FA Cup Final
Saturday, 14 May 2011
Attendance: 88,643

City: Hart, Richards, Kompany, Lescott, Kolarov, de Jong, Barry (Johnson), Toure, David Silva (Vieira), Balotelli, Tevez (Zabaleta) [**Toure**]

Manager: Roberto Mancini

Stoke City: Sorensen, Wilkinson, Shawcross, Huth, Wilson, Pennant, Whelan (Pugh), Delap (Carew), Etherington (Whitehead), Jones, Walters.

ROBERTO MANCINI had vowed to change history, but even he must have surely known that only the Russians, the Chinese, the North Koreans and few other powerful regimes can do that.

Instead, the Italian changed the future as the Blues rubbed away 35 years of hurt, landing the club's first trophy since Dennis Tueart's memorable bicycle kick had beaten Newcastle in the League Cup Final at the old Wembley back in 1976.

Here at the new Wembley, Yaya Toure, as he had been in the semi-final win in this same competition (see Chapter 24), sealed a memorable success with a memorable goal.

The crucial, match-winning moment came on 74 minutes when Silva, who had turned on the proverbial sixpence, and Balotelli combined brilliantly inside the Stoke box. The latter's shot was blocked, but the loose ball came out to Toure, whose powerful shot gave Thomas Sorensen in the Stoke goal no chance whatsoever.

In fact, Toure's left-footed strike was way too close to the keeper, but there was so much power, almost venom, behind it that it was in the back of the net in the blink of an eye.

The Blues had been the better side throughout and no one – not even the Stoke fans who sportingly stayed behind to applaud the City team at the finish – could gainsay that.

Sorensen might have conceded more, but did brilliantly to keep out a number of good efforts, particularly one from the mercurial Balotelli, who was voted Man of the Match. Had the Danish keeper been on the winning side, it's arguable that he might have clinched that award for himself.

Stoke's best chance came in the second half when Kenwyne Jones found himself one-on-one with Hart, but the City stopper spread himself well enough to keep out the effort. It was their only shot on target over the 90 minutes and once they had gone behind, they reverted to their long-ball game without troubling the City defence too much.

MARIO'S VERDICT The eccentric Mario Balotelli when asked 'was that your best performance in a Manchester City shirt?' responded by blowing a kiss to the would-be interviewer. Eventually he tells his interrogator: "My season was shit."

CAPTAIN CARLOS Tevez, who had missed the semi-final success through injury, stepped up to receive the trophy as City skipper from Prime Minister David Cameron.

TREADING ON TRADITION? Well almost, as for the first time in many years, the Cup Final wasn't the only game of the day. There were a number of Premier League fixtures being played during the afternoon. Back in the pre-war era, it happened all the time. In fact, on the day City were getting hammered 3-0 by Dixie Dean's Everton in the 1933 Final, there were nine First Division matches, while in the Second Division that day, Manchester United were losing 3-2 at Lincoln City (thought I'd slip that one in).

GUARDIAN ANGEL Daniel Taylor, writing in *The Guardian*, summed it all up after the final whistle: "It was the moment Manchester City had craved for longer than they will care to remember, the day they could release all that pent-up frustration. The long, sometimes brutal wait for a trophy is finally over."

DEJA VU ALL OVER AGAIN! For the second time in a big game at Wembley against City, the Stoke manager Tony Pulis was on the losing side. He was in charge of the Gillingham team that lost the Second Division Play-Off Final 12 years earlier.

PULIS PRAISE Tony Pulis was full of praise for the Stoke fans, saying: "For our supporters to stay behind and clap Manchester City was a great gesture, and they should take credit for that. To watch the other club pick up the trophy is pretty unique."

NO DELAP OF HONOUR There was no lap of honour for Stoke long throw specialist and Republic of Ireland international Rory Delap, but his son Liam joined City after ten years at Derby County's youth academy. The promising striker made his first team debut for City against AFC Bournemouth in the League Cup, scoring in the 15th minute of a 2-1 home win in September 2020. Three days later, he made his Premier League debut, coming on as a sub in the 5-2 home defeat by Leicester City.

SWASHBUCKLING STOKE You don't normally associate the word "swashbuckling" with Stoke, but that's how the team was described in a Cup Final preview by local paper, the *Stoke Sentinel* prior to the Final. Here's the full quote: "It was a golden, swashbuckling spring of 2011 for Stoke City. The Tony Pulis era peaked with a brilliantly-balanced team; hard and athletic with no little skill."

CLASS ACT The two teams were actually scheduled to play a Premier League fixture on the day of the Final, but they didn't meet in the League until the following Tuesday. And even though it was City's final home game of the season the club's hierarchy decided not to show off the FA Cup out of respect for the visiting Stoke fans. City won 3-0 and waited for another week before they staged an open-top bus parade through the streets of Manchester to celebrate their Wembley win.

Chapter 26

AGUEROOO – A LIFE-CHANGING MOMENT

City 3 Queens Park Rangers 2
Etihad Stadium
Premier League
Sunday 13 May 2012
Attendance: 47,435

City: Hart, Kompany, Zabaleta, Lescott, Clichy, Barry (Dzeko), Nasri, Silva, Y Toure (de Jong), Aguero, Tevez (Balotelli). [**Zabaleta, Dzeko, Aguero**]

Manager: Roberto Mancini

Queens Park Rangers: Kenny, Hill, Taiwo, Ferdinand, Onuoha, Derry, Barton, Wright-Phillips, Mackie, Cisse (Traore), Zamora (Bothroyd). [**Cisse, Mackie**]

WITH the 90 minutes up and City 2-1 down in the club's most important game since the Gillingham Play-off Final at Wembley, it was time to hit the pause button.

So, switching off the mobile phone as well, I took a stroll around the garden to try to calm my shredded nerves.

I was walking up and down like a Zombie for about five minutes before plucking up the courage to put the TV back on.

By then, of course, the drama was over.

Two minutes after I had re-started the game, Dzeko soared high above the QPR defence to make it 2-2 from a corner.

It was a lifeline, but no more than that. United were winning 1-0 at Sunderland with only three minutes left on the clock, so they were in pole position to hang on to their title.

At the Stadium of Light, it had gone dark for the Blues as the final whistle signalled a United win after three minutes of stoppage time had been played out.

City were still out there; still straining every sinew; still hoping, but many fans were in anguish as it looked as though we'd blown our chance.

Then, the Aguerooo moment changed all our lives forever.

The Argentinean received a pass from de Jong on the edge of the QPR box, touched it on to Balotelli, who seemed to stumble as he turned. But even as the Italian fell, he managed to get the ball to Aguero who had sprinted past him.

We were three minutes-plus into added time as Aguero received the ball, QPR's Tase Taiwo threw himself into a tackle. He did seem to make contact and perhaps on another day Sergio might have gone to ground. But not this time.

The angle wasn't the best, but Aguero still managed to power his shot past Paddy Kenny.

Cue delirium.

Life as a City fan was never the same again.

In my humble opinion, there were four key moments in this momentous match:

1.   Lescott's misjudgement of a long ball through the middle, which led to QPR's equaliser.

2.   The sending-off of QPR's ex-City player Joey Barton.

3.   Dzeko's equaliser at 2-2.

4.   Aguero's match-winner. Obviously.

Zabaleta, a man who would have willingly run through a brick wall for the club he loved so much, put us ahead when the QPR keeper, later to play an absolute blinder, made a bit of a hash of the full-back's shot.

Nineteen minutes earlier Wayne Rooney had put United ahead at Sunderland, so Zab's goal put us back on top of the Premiership table on goal difference.

But it all went dark again when Djibril Cisse took advantage of an error by Lescott and stunned the majority of the Etihad crowd with an equaliser. United were now two points clear at the top with 42 "normal" minutes of the season remaining.

Then Barton sees red in the 55th minute, but despite that body blow, the west Londoners go ahead 11 minutes later through Jamie Mackie. There are just 24 minutes – and the clock is ticking. Fast.

United are now three points ahead in the title race.

But City never stopped going forward, willed on by fans who were now in turmoil.

Balotelli is sent on by Mancini and the rest is Man City history.

Dzeko makes it 2-2 before Aguero's never-to-be-forgotten goal seals victory.

And breathe...

What made it that much sweeter was the look on Alex Ferguson's face and the look on the United players' and fans' faces up on Wearside as the news of City's victory filtered through.

PLAYING IT BY THE BOOK Aguero was booked for taking off his shirt after scoring the sensational winner, although I didn't see it at the time nor did anyone else, I suspect. Rules is rules, I suppose, and Mike Dean had no hesitation in reaching for his yellow card amidst the mayhem. I hope he got Aguero to sign it for him afterwards...

DOUBLE CELEBRATION Although Rangers fans went wild when Mackie gave them the lead midway through the second half, in the end they didn't actually need to win. Their relegation fears were put to rest when Bolton failed to beat Stoke ensuring the London side's Premiership survival. So, there was the rare sight of both sets of fans joyously happy at the final whistle.

STATS RIGHT Had City not triumphed it would have been a mathematical travesty according to the stats. The Blues won the shot count 44-3 with a 15-3 success on target and a 10-0 win off target. City blocked no QPR shots, while the visitors managed to get in the way of an astonishing 19 City efforts. Corners was a walkover at 19-0 and our successful passes rate was just over 91 per cent.

HINDSIGHT'S A WONDERFUL ASSET Commentator Martin Tyler, famous for his Aguerooo moment, claimed 10 years later: "The only thing I've ever been able to remember about that day with clarity is that the moment Sergio took a touch, I knew he'd score."

He added: "I've no reason for saying what I did when he did score and people have often suggested I must have had something up my sleeve, but how can you even imagine a scenario like that?

"Saying what I said when he did score just enabled me to draw breath I suppose because I just knew having played football and coached football what would happen because it was him.

"Lesser mortals would have snatched at the chance, but he was the right person at the right moment for Manchester City and that's the only explanation I can give for what happened actually happening."

During the game and with just five minutes left on the clock, Tyler had told viewers: "If they [City] win the title from here I don't think it will ever be topped."

ON THE MARK According to Tyler, former City manager Mark Hughes, in charge of QPR, said later that evening that Aguero's goal produced "the noisiest moment in a football ground he had ever heard".

FERGIE'S WISH Speaking on the eve of the game, the United manager said: "You just hope something stupid happens." Joey Barton?

THREE REDS AND YOU'RE OUT Paul Merson, speaking on Sky

Sports, reckoned Barton could have received three red cards. Merson claimed that the ex-City man could have been sent off for kicking out at Aguero and then trying to head butt Kompany after initially tangling with Tevez. In the end, Micah Richards persuaded Barton to get off the field before he caused any more mayhem.

Chapter 27

FIGHTING A LOSING BATTLE AT BARCA

Barcelona 2 City 1
Nou Camp
Champions League Round of 16
Wednesday 12 March 2014
Attendance: 88,626

Barcelona: Valdes, Alves, Pique, Maschereno, Alba, Xavi, Busquets, Iniesta, Messi, Fabregas (Roberto), Neymar (Sanchez). *[**Messi, Alves**]*

City: Hart, Zabaleta, Kompany, Lescott, Kolarov, Silva (Negredo), Fernandinho, Milner, Nasri (Navas), Y Toure, Aguero (Dzeko). [**Kompany**]

Manager: Manuel Pellegrini

YOU'RE 2-0 down from the first leg, having been outplayed, and the return is at the Nou Camp in front of around 85,000 baying Barcelonians.

Add in to this heady Catalan cocktail the fact that the Blues had conceded two away goals at the Etihad and were making their first appearance in the competition's knockout stages against one of Europe's superpowers, and you might be forgiven for not bothering to attend.

Not so.

I'd paid my air fare, booked a hotel room and secured a match ticket.

Three good-ish reasons to hotfoot it to Spain.

So here I was in the famous stadium, which truth be told was quite shabby in the parts that I saw. I'm sure the Barcelona bourgeoisie are housed in relative luxury in the comfort of their expensive seats, but up here in the rarefied atmosphere of the Nou Camp's top shelf it was a little less salubrious.

In fact, I was told on fairly good authority that the Barcelona stewards were all former Sherpas doing some off-season work before returning to the Himalayas!

But back to the game.

Well, in summary we gave it a good go, but were never able to match Barca. In the first half the incomparable Messi hit a post and several other chances for the home side to increase their stranglehold on the tie went begging as Hart proved our star performer.

We were by no means passive though and were on the front foot for large parts of the first 45 minutes, even though the home side managed to carve out several really good chances.

In the home leg, City had probably been overawed by a combination of Barca's skill and determination.

I was actually taken aback by how quickly Barcelona players retrieved the ball when they lost it, hunting in packs of two or three, and how well they looked after the ball when they had it – probably a blueprint for the way the Blues now play under Guardiola.

Here in this second leg, Neymar did manage to beat Hart in the first-half, but Alba was adjudged offside, although action replays showed that the referee might have erred.

And we rode our luck again when Lescott got away with what looked like a foul inside the area on Messi very early on.

Lescott was again in the thick of things when he gave away possession in the first half and Messi (again) took advantage only to strike the post.

And just before the break Fernandinho kicked one off the line; this time a Neymar shot after Messi had cut through City's defence.

City were coming off a shock defeat by Wigan Athletic in the FA Cup quarter-finals the previous weekend, but were still determined to take the game to Barca when they could.

But when Lescott (again) failed to cut out a Fabregas pass, that man Messi was on hand to make it 1-0 on the night, 3-0 on aggregate.

And with Aguero off injured and replaced by Dzeko, the cause looked well lost although it was Dzeko who brought out the save of the night from Valdez after climbing above Pique to send a header towards the top corner.

We continued to go forward and felt we might have had a spot kick after Pique's challenge on Dzeko but seconds later things got even worse when Zabaleta – already in the referee's notebook for an earlier foul – saw red after vigorously protesting the decision.

Even with 10 men, the Blues managed to pull one back when Kompany tapped in from close range after following up Dzeko's flick with a minute left. The City skipper looked offside but replays showed that he was being played on by Barcelona defender Sergi Roberto.

Ultimately, Barcelona had the final say when in added time, they exploited the space left by City at the back and Alves, who also scored late on at the Etihad, squeezed a shot over the line from Iniesta's pass.

DODGY DECISIONS Dan Ripley in the *Daily Mail* wrote: "City will be fuming over that penalty claim not given, but Barcelona had a few dodgy decisions go against them too in what was a nightmare evening for the match officials who got many big calls wrong."

CAPTAIN'S COMMENTS Kompany said: "We've nothing left in the tank. We gave everything out there."

RED MIST Zabaleta's dismissal was the 26th recorded for an opponent of Barcelona and the tenth for an English side against the Catalans – both Champions League records.

SEVEN-UP Barcelona reached the Champions League quarter-finals for the seventh straight season.

Chapter 28

SO CLOSE TO THE TITLE

City 4 Aston Villa 0
Premier League
Etihad Stadium
Wednesday, 7 May 2014
Attendance: 47,023

City: Hart, Zabaleta, Kompany, Demichelis, Kolarov, Garcia, Toure, Milner (Jovetic), Silva (Fernandinho), Nasri, Dzeko (Negredo). [**Dzeko 2, Jovetic, Toure**]

Manager: Manuel Pellegrini

Aston Villa: Guzan, Lowton, Vlaar, Baker, Clark (Robinson), El Ahmadi, Westwood, Delph, Weinmann, Bowery (Bacuna), Bertrand (Grealish).

IT WASN'T the most important goal of perhaps the most important game of the season.

But it was the most emphatic and summed up the relentless pressure that City had exerted – not only on Aston Villa – but on the rest of the Premier League as the Blues drove themselves on almost dementedly to another elite-level title.

After Toure's goal had put the icing on the celebration cake, City needed just a draw in their final game of the season against West Ham to take the crown. There was nothing that second-placed Liverpool could do. It was out of their hands.

Fittingly the scorer, in the third minute of added time of the 90, was Yaya Toure who summed up, in a pulsating run from inside his own half exactly that never-say-die spirit and determination that City had shown throughout a long, tough season.

Toure, in his prime, had an amazing engine and once on a roll was always enormously difficult to shrug off.

Here, in driving rain on a sodden surface, Toure just kept on rolling with tired Villa defenders trailing in his wake like tiny tugs chasing a giant container ship on speed.

For such a big man, Yaya was always capable of an exquisite touch or two and this time he skilfully clipped the ball past Brad Guzan, who by then must have been sick of the sight of the City attack which had already breached Villa's defences three times even without the injured Aguero, who was out with a groin problem.

As Paul Doyle wrote of Toure's goal in *The Guardian*: "You have to say that's magnificent. No other player in the league can do that. Toure collected the ball in his own half and then romped past two defenders with a unique blend of power and finesses before delicately clipping the ball past the out-rushing Guzan and into the net. Simply wonderful."

And Alan Shearer told BBC viewers: "Yaya Toure is a machine. He did not have one of his better games but what he did, he did very well.

"His fourth goal was like watching a 15-year-old against under-12s. You just can't catch him. He is only the second midfielder to score 20 goals or more after Frank Lampard in the Premier League."

And how right both of them were.

But early on in the piece, frustration covered the Etihad like a giant umbrella as the rain, picked out by the floodlights, poured down in almost biblical proportions.

My seat, booked only at the very last minute, was high up in the

MATCH 7: COLIN BELL WATCHES AS HIS SHOT BEATS SPURS
KEEPER PAT JENNINGS, CYRIL KNOWLES AND ALAN MULLERY

MATCH 15: NICKY WEAVER
GOES CRAZY AT THE END
OF THE PENALTY SHOOT- OUT

MATCH 26: AGUEROOO'S LATE LATE TITLE CLINCHER

MATCH 28: EDIN DZEKO OPENS
THE SCORING AGAINST VILLA

MATCH 29: TRIUMPHANT SCENES AT THE END OF THE 2016 CAPITAL ONE CUP FINAL

MATCH 32: LEROY SANE WITH THE WINNER AGAINST LIVERPOOL

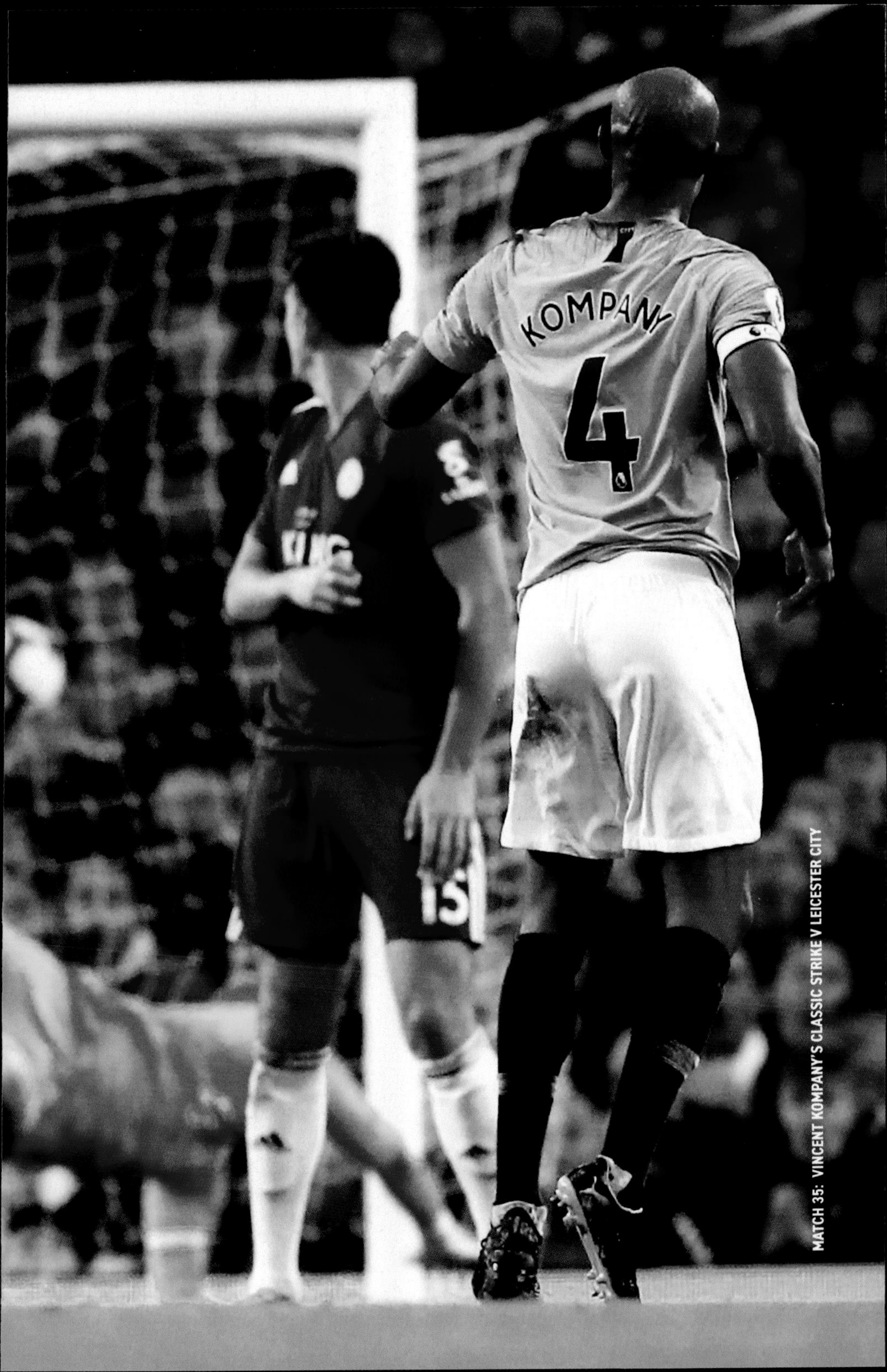

MATCH 35: VINCENT KOMPANY'S CLASSIC STRIKE V LEICESTER CITY

MATCH 37: GABRIEL JESUS
CELEBRATES SCORING THE FIRST GOAL
IN MADRID WITH RIYAD MAHREZ

MATCH 46: KEVIN DE BRUYNE IS MOBBED BY TEAMMATES AFTER NETTING THE FIRST AT PSG

MATCH 48: SERGIO AGUERO SIGNS OFF WITH THE PREMIER LEAGUE TITLE

third tier of the Colin Bell Stand – so high that the steward checking my ticket looked sympathetic as he showed me to my perch..

When I finally reached my eyrie, I asked the guy sitting on my left to let me know if we scored. He promised he would.

It was deep into the match before either of us had anything to cheer about.

That moment of sheer relief came in the 63rd minute when Dzeko finally broke the deadlock after Kompany (twice, once with an uncharacteristic overhead kick), Silva and Nasri had all gone close.

Dzeko made it look as simple as it was when he got on the end of a typical Zabaleta overlap.

And the Bosnian doubled the advantage with help from Zabaleta again and Nasri.

Horrifyingly, Villa almost hit back when Weinmann and Bowery combined. Thankfully, the latter could only turn the ball into the side netting.

But the game was made safe – if it wasn't already – when that man Toure did some superb work around the edge of the penalty area to set up Jovetic for a goal that had the scoreboards flashing 3-0.

And then, of course, Toure turned from provider to producer to make it 4-0 in his own unforgettable style.

GREALISH MAKES HIS DEBUT AT THE ETIHAD Eighteen-year-old Jack Grealish came on with three minutes left to make his Premier League debut for Villa. Can't say I really noticed the boy or that he made much difference to the visitors' performance. Quite the reverse; they were only 2-0 down when he made it onto the field. At the time, Grealish was an Irish Under-21 international and was described by an Irish sports website as "a hugely talented teenager".

STATS THE WAY TO DO IT There are lies, damned lies and football stats, but the figures from this game do tell an accurate story of City's dominance. Possession was at 73 per cent, the shot count was 18-5 in our favour, with the Blues shots on target tally at nine and Villa's precisely nil.

PELLEGRINI'S FORECAST In his post-match press comments Pellegrini said he expected City to clinch the Premier title on the Sunday after this game – and he was spot on as they beat West Ham 2-0 to seal the deal. Summing up the League campaign so far, he said: "It has been a strange season because we have never been at the top of the table. Everybody was talking about us being the favourites but in March we were nine points behind Liverpool and eight behind Chelsea. We had three games in hand but we had to win all of those games. Now we are top and I hope we are not going to lose on Sunday, but we must play the way we have played against Villa, and the way we have played all season. It is difficult to find just one key moment in the season. The most important thing is that this team has always believed we can win the title."

Chapter 29

MANUEL GETS IT RIGHT, RIGHT, RIGHT

City 1 Liverpool 1
(after extra-time; City won 3-1 on penalties)
Wembley Stadium
League Cup Final
Sunday 28 February 2016
Attendance: 86,206

City: Caballero, Sagna (Zabaleta), Kompany, Otamendi, Clichy, Y Toure, Fernando (Navas), Fernandinho, Silva (Bony), Sterling, Aguero. [**Fernandinho**]

Manager: Manuel Pellegrini

Liverpool: Mignolet, Clyne, Lucas, Sakho (K Toure), Moreno (Lallana), Milner, Henderson, Can, Coutinho, Firmino (Origi), Sturridge. [**Coutinho**]

THE connection between goalkeeper Willy Caballero and manager Manuel Pellegrini was strong.

The decision by the boss to stick with the keeper in a big final was contentious.

But Pellegrini, who had coached Caballero at Malaga, was proved right, right, right when the City stopper did just that, saving penalties from Lucas, Philippe Coutinho and Adam Lallana in a dramatic shoot-out finale.

Yet even prior to his shoot-out heroics, Caballero had made the save of the match when keeping out a Divock Origi header in the 108th minute.

Surprisingly, Pellers stuck with Caballero over Hart despite the Argentine's dreadful display in the 5-1 FA Cup fifth round thrashing by Chelsea a week earlier when City had fielded a substantially under-strength side.

Fernandinho, who had put City ahead early in the first half when Liverpool keeper Simon Mignolet could well have done much better, was the first to go for the Blues in the penalty kicks decider after Can had put Liverpool 1-0 up.

However, the Brazilian who had probably been fortunate with his goal, had no such luck from the spot, striking the post.

Thankfully, Navas and Aguero both fired home as Caballero was donning his Superman outfit to make his three decisive stops, leaving Yaya Toure to score the winner, making absolutely no mistake as he sent City fans into raptures.

Beating Liverpool, after all, had never been a regular occurrence in my lifetime – or many other people's lifetimes.

It was a strange sight when that penalty hit the back of the net as Toure wheeled away in triumph – alone. In normal circumstances he would have been mobbed, but the City players and support staff ran straight towards Caballero on the touchline before some of them joined Toure, who had stripped off his shirt in celebration.

Of course, all this might have been avoided had Sterling not missed two gilt-edged (or was it guilt-edged?) opportunities with the Blues 1-0 ahead. Even the normally deadly Aguero struck a post and was wide with another effort, all of which left the way open for Coutinho to level the scores with only seven minutes remaining of normal time.

Cue an additional 30 minutes which failed to end the stalemate, leaving penalties as the final option.

Fans from both sides, as well the "corporates" who occupied some of the more prestigious seats, couldn't complain about the entertainment on show over the 120 minutes plus the time it took for penalties.

Spot kicks apart, there were 36 shots with 11 of them on target. Liverpool won both those head-to-head duels in the stats department, but on actual play, City generally served up the better football with Silva pulling the strings in midfield and definitely had more clear-cut chances.

BOO BOYS TARGET RAHEEM Sterling, a hated figure among the Anfield faithful after his contentious £49 million transfer from the Merseyside club, was booed every time he touched the ball.

CITY OLD BOYS ON A LOSER Three ex-City players, James Milner, Daniel Sturridge and Kolo Toure, who replaced the injured Sakho in the first half, ended up on the losing side. Kolo, who was playing against his younger brother Yaya, is now a first team coach at Leicester City.

NO COMMENT NEEDED I found this on YouTube after watching the highlights of the final. It was put up by Shaun McGinnity in February 2021 and I have no idea whether he's a City fan or a neutral: "Never had an issue with Liverpool till this day. The two service-station stops on the way down changed that. The hatred, the bile and the f*****g arrogance of them Liverpool fans we met that day has left me always looking for their results hoping they get beat." I feel no further comment is needed.

WINNING GOODBYE FOR PELLEGRINI This was City's final trophy win before Pep Guardiola took over in the following season. Manuel Pellegrini, dubbed 'This Charming Man' by Blues fans, also steered the club into the Champions League semi-finals and into fourth place in the Premier League. The much-travelled Chilean had completed the Premier League-League Cup double two seasons earlier.

FINALLY PAYING THE PENALTY This was only the fourth time that Liverpool had lost a penalty shoot-out – having faced 18 in total. They had previously won all five cup finals that had been decided on penalties

MAN OF THE MATCH Vincent Kompany earned that accolade,

making only his third start of the season after being out with a calf injury that had kept him on the sidelines for three months.

LIVERPOOL'S REVENGE Three days later the two teams met at Anfield in the Premier League, where Liverpool gained some measure of revenge, beating us 3-0.

Chapter 30

FOOTBALL'S VERSION OF HELL

City 1 Liverpool 2
(Liverpool won 5-1 on aggregate)
Champions League Quarter-final
Etihad Stadium
Tuesday, 10 April 2018
Attendance: 53,461

City: Ederson, Walker, Otamendi, Laporte, Fernandinho, De Bruyne, Silva (Aguero), Sane, Sterling, Bernardo (Gundogan), Jesus. [**Jesus**]

Manager: Pep Guardiola

Liverpool: Karius, Alexander-Arnold (Clyne), Lovren, van Dijk, Roberston, Oxlade-Chamberlain, Wijnaldum, Milner, Salah (Ings), Firmino (Klavan), Mane. [**Salah, Firmino**]

FOR 45 minutes, City unleashed a footballing hell on Liverpool. They scored in the second minute, hit the post, and a had a "goal" incorrectly ruled out for offside. Oh, and we had a couple of those 'I've seen them given' penalty appeals turned down.

Then, to cap one of the most frenetic first half displays I have ever seen, they had manager Pep Guardiola sent to the stands for his wild-eyed protests over the aforementioned offside decision.

That was the moment we lost this tie although in reality we had lost almost all hope after a 3-0 defeat at Anfield a week earlier.

MANCHESTER CITY – 50 MEMORABLE MATCHES

But when have football fans been realistic? Had we gone in at the interval 2-0 up and with Pep still on the touchline for the second half, who knows.

The footballing gods deserted us that night, whereas our footballing brains had deserted us on Merseyside.

The opening half will long live in my memory as City, with the crowd as switched on as the players, put the Liverpool defence to the sword. The Scousers in the crowd had to look away as their team was pushed back time and again.

On two minutes, we had pulled a goal back when Jesus swept the ball home after Sterling had robbed Virgil Van Dijk.

A precision De Bruyne pass put Sterling in the clear and again he found Jesus, but the Brazilian couldn't get his shot away.

The two penalty appeals came and went with the TV commentary team confirming that Spanish referee Antonio Miguel Mateu Lahoz got it right on both occasions. City fans didn't think so.

Bernardo was here, there and everywhere, and was unlucky to strike the post with Loris Karius in the Liverpool goal a long way from the ball five minutes before the break.

But that heart-breaking moment was soon forgotten when it looked as though Sane had made it 2-0 – and only a goal down in the tie – almost on half-time.

It was, however, chalked off, even though the ball had come to Sane from one our very own, James Milner, now of course wearing the red of Liverpool, on its way past the keeper.

Up in the stands, a long way off admittedly, it looked as though Milner had inadvertently steered the ball to Sane, but I don't blame the linesman/referee's assistant. There was no way he could have seen from his side-on position.

But the ref should have spotted it – he's paid to make such split-second decision. Instead, he decided 'no goal' and 'no Pep' after the Catalan had forcibly put his case as the teams left the field at the break.

There was no sense we had given up even without Guardiola urging us on from pitchside, but Mo Salah, who had been an injury doubt beforehand, made it 1-1 on the night with a 56th minute goal before Roberto Firmino took advantage of the "error-waiting-to-happen" style of Otamendi to nip in to score Liverpool's second.

We went close a few times and Gundogan had a "goal" disallowed for offside, but it mattered not a jot with Liverpool sealing a 5-1 aggregate win.

UNWANTED HAT-TRICK It was City's third successive defeat after losses to Liverpool in the first leg the previous week and against Manchester United at the weekend. That meant Guardiola had lost three consecutive matches in all competitions for the first time since May 2015 when he was Bayern Munich's boss.

WHAT THEY SAID The Times: "For 45 minutes City were thrillingly bold. You always suspected that there would be a price to pay in second-half raggedness. To play at that tempo, teetering between brilliance and desperation was never going to be sustainable."

UEFA reporter Simon Hart: "For City this capped the worst week of their season – a third straight defeat and the very worst time to hit a blip. It might, just might, have been different had they got a second goal before the break. Pep Guardiola had set them up in a bold formation and after the excitement of their early goal, they were close to making it 2-0 in the final minutes of the half with Sane's offside goal and Bernardo Silva striking a post.

"It was impossible to sustain their high tempo in the second half, though. They were not at their incisive best, and as the belief ebbed and energy levels dropped, Liverpool picked them off."

The **Manchester Evening News**: "Bernardo Silva was quite brilliant, giving Liverpool all kinds of difficulties down their left, and reposing the question of why he did not start at Anfield."

STATS A SHAME City were ahead on shots (20-5), passes (646-309) and possession (69%-31%), but, unfortunately, not on goals and that's all that really matters at the end of the day.

Chapter 31

BLUES BOUNCE BACK

Tottenham Hotspur 1 City 3
Wembley Stadium
Premier League
Saturday, 14 April 2018
Attendance: 80,811

Tottenham Hotspur: Loris, Trippier, Sanchez, Vertonghen, Davies, Dembele (Moura), Dier, Lamela (Son), Eriksen, Alli (Sissoko), Kane. [**Eriksen**]

City: Ederson, Walker, Kompany, Laporte, Delph, De Bruyne (Toure), Gundogan, Silva, Sterling, Jesus (Bernardo), Sane (Otamendi). [**Jesus, Gundogan** pen, **Sterling**]

Manager: Pep Guardiola

ONLY four days after their heart-breaking Champions League quarter-final exit against Liverpool and a week after an agonising collapse against United, City picked themselves up off the floor to move within three points of the Premier League title after this stirring win against Spurs.

Travelling to Spurs' temporary home as the north London side awaited the opening of their new Tottenham Hotspur Stadium, was a daunting task for a side who had given their all in a frenetic Champions League defeat by Liverpool.

And it wasn't only the Liverpool defeat that might have been preying on City's minds; the weekend before they had totally dominated United in the derby at the Etihad, going in at half time 2-0 ahead (and it should have been more) only to fold dramatically in the second half, losing 3-2.

Added into the mix was Spurs' improved form; the side hadn't suffered a League defeat since losing to City a couple of weeks before Christmas, an unbeaten run of 14 games.

City carried on where they left off against United as they swarmed all over Spurs with Silva and De Bruyne being afforded the freedom of Wembley's wide-open spaces.

And just three minutes in Sane hit the post with a volley with Lloris well beaten. What a start that would have been in such an important game.

So, it was a relief when in the 22nd minute, Jesus opened the scoring, latching onto a long, punted ball from Kompany before sliding a low shot past Lloris.

Three minutes after those Jesus goal celebrations, we were ecstatic again when referee John Moss pointed to the penalty spot after Lloris had slid into Sterling. What we didn't know at the time – and couldn't see from the opposite end of the ground – was that the keeper's challenge was just outside the area and, thankfully, about 16 months before VAR's introduction.

Ice-cool Ilkay Gundogan stepped up to hammer the ball past the France keeper and it was 2-0.

What could go wrong?

A fortuitous goal against the run of play?

Well, yes.

And it was Christian Eriksen who provided it as he raced onto a through ball from Harry Kane and his shot hit Laporte before rebounding back to the Dane, who stuck it past Ederson.

Guardiola wasn't amused, throwing down his water bottle in disgust at his side's defensive frailties.

To use a well-known darts phrase that seems to have been hi-jacked by TV's football commentators, it was 'game on'.

Buoyed by their goal, Spurs came out for the second half all hustle and bustle, and for a time, the Blues defence was forced, to well, defend

But 72 minutes in all that pressure was relieved – and it was Jesus and Sterling to the fore again as the Brazilian's shot was parried by Lloris only as far as the England man who gleefully swallowed up the opportunity.

Eighteen minutes plus a little stoppage time later we had secured our first win in four games.

WHAT THE MANAGERS SAID Pep Guardiola: "I said to my staff after 10-15 minutes 'After today we will be champions.' After the last week to come here and play like we did, we will be champions.

"In the past with [defeats by] Manchester United and Liverpool, maybe it was not easy for the players but we were good and we created chances in the second half to score more goals and we're so happy.

"We will try hard to be champions in front of our fans at the Etihad Stadium."

Spurs **Mauricio Pochettino**: "In the end, if we analyse the game, they fully deserve the victory. For sure they are going to win the league, but I'm disappointed because we didn't compete in the first 25 minutes."

DID YOU KNOW? City became only the fourth side to have won at Arsenal, Chelsea and Spurs in a Premier League campaign, joining some unlikely bedfellows, Coventry (1993-94), Charlton (2001-02) and Blackburn (2002-03).

BY JESUS! The oft-criticised Jesus brought his season's goal involvement to 27 goals in 34 starts in all competitions (20 goals and seven assists).

PENALTY FAMINE Gundogan's penalty was the first Spurs had conceded in 59 Premier League fixtures.

Chapter 32

THE TURNING POINT

City 2 Liverpool 1
Etihad Stadium
Premier League
Thursday 3 January 2019
Attendance: 54,511

City: Ederson, Danilo, Stones. Kompany (Otamendi), Laporte (Walker), Bernardo, Fernandinho, Silva (Gundogan), Sterling, Aguero, Sane. [**Aguero, Sane**]

Manager: Pep Guardiola

Liverpool: Alisson, Alexander-Arnold, Lovren, van Dijk, Robertson. Wijnaldum (Sturridge), Henderson, Milner (Fabinho), Salah, Firmino, Mane (Shaqiri). [**Firmino**]

'THIS is it, the most important game of the season'. How many times have you heard that phrase fall from the lips of a fan or from one of the game's legion of pundits?

But even without the benefit of hindsight, this really *was* the biggest game of the 2018-19 campaign. A seminal moment. The turning point.

We were seven points behind Jurgen Klopp's well-oiled gegenpressing machine and defeat here would leave us 10 points behind and the title dream almost shattered. Victory, on the other hand, would see us right back in it, just four points behind with all to play for.

I don't think anyone had mentioned the possibility of a draw. Pep didn't play for draws, certainly not at home. He'd always been too greedy, too hungry for success to share the points. He'd even gone on record beforehand saying that anything other than a win wasn't an option.

Right from the off, the tempo was high, the atmosphere febrile, almost frantic. The sound and the fury.

But one player kept his cool in that almost fast-forward 45 minutes – one Sergio Aguero, who in 2012, of course, had had his own seminal moment with that never-to-be-forgotten title-clinching goal against QPR.

Here he was, seven years on from *that moment*, scoring a fabulous goal, from what looked to us mere mortals, an impossible angle.

The sheer ferocity of Aguero's strike as it beat Allison at his near post, was entirely in keeping with the no-holds-barred first half.

Aguero's goal made that half-time cuppa even sweeter, but talk about fine margins as prior to City taking the lead, Liverpool came within 1.12 centimetres – less than half an inch – of snatching the first goal.

Salah was heavily involved in a fluid move which saw Mane strike the inside of the post; Stones scrambled to clear and, in the process, only managed to crash the ball against Ederson and it looped back on its way into the net. But incredibly, Stones managed to recover to clear it off the line and through the legs of the onrushing Salah.

The referee's watch confirmed it hadn't gone in.

In the earlier exchanges, Kompany might easily have seen red – he probably did in his own mind when he went in for the tackle – after a lunge on Salah that Klopp claimed should have resulted in the City skipper's dismissal.

On the other side of the ledger, Virgil van Dijk clobbered Aguero as Liverpool sought desperately to preserve their 20-game unbeaten start to the PL season, which was threatening our 22-match unbeaten start the previous season.

So, we went in at the interval with a 1-0 lead and that goal which came five minutes before the break, must presumably have changed the nature of Herr Klopp's half-time team talk.

But whatever was said in the away dressing room had the desired effect when on 64 minutes Firmino scored with a stooping header after both Liverpool full-backs had been involved, with Alexander-Arnold's cross finding Robertson on the other flank before the latter headed it on to Firmino, who gave Ederson no chance.

It was back into the melting pot and for a time Liverpool looked as though they might grab a second, but City, inspired by Fernandinho's iron-like grip on the midfield, gradually wrested the initiative from the Merseysiders and with 18 minutes left on the clock, Leroy Sane proved himself the hero.

Sane took the ball in his stride from Raheem Sterling's pass and the German's beautifully-controlled left-foot shot skimmed across Allison and went in off the far post.

On 82 minutes, Sterling broke free on the halfway line and fed Aguero, who went round Alisson only to see the Brazilian divert the shot wide with an outstretched hand.

Sterling himself might have made it 3-1 soon afterwards, shooting wide with Allison scampering across his line.

Bang on 90 minutes and Bernardo wriggled free and fired in a shot that Alisson could only beat out – straight to Sterling, whose powerful shot was wide.

In the final stages, Liverpool battled back, using long-ball tactics in the main to discomfit the City defence, but the Blues just about held it all together to celebrate a momentous victory as Anthony Taylor blew the final whistle after five nerve-shredding minutes of added time.

HOME BOY Sane's match-winner brought his Etihad record to 26 goal involvements in 25 games since the start of the previous season (nine goals, 17 assists).

BIG PLAYER Since the start of the 2011-12 season, Aguero had scored 37 league goals for City in matches against the other 'big six' clubs

(Arsenal, Chelsea, Liverpool, Manchester United and Tottenham) – 16 more than any other player.

MANAGERS' VERDICTS Guardiola: "I am proud of them, but not just today. We lost two games in four days but you can't forget what they have done for 16 months. We knew that it was a final today, if we lose it is almost over." **Klopp**: "It was a big pressure. Very intense game. We were unlucky in our finishing moments. Unluckier than City I would say."

NOT NEEDED City won despite not calling on brilliant Belgian Kevin De Bruyne, who was an unused substitute.

IRONIC? *The Guardian*'s match reporter on the night, Barney Ronay, tweeted after it was all over: "Great to see Man City finally maturing past the fancy passing style into a proper last-ditch defence shanked-clearance hoofball team. I predict great success with this new look."

Chapter 33

CHELSEA'S CAR CRASH MOMENT

City 0 Chelsea 0
(after extra time; City won 4-3 on penalties)
Wembley Stadium
Carabao Cup Final
Sunday 24 February 2019
Attendance: 81,775

City: Ederson, Walker, Otamendi, Laporte (Kompany), Zinchenko, De Bruyne (Sane), Fernandinho (Danilo), Silva (Gundogan), Bernardo, Agüero, Sterling.

Manager: Pep Guardiola

Chelsea: Arrizabalaga, Azpilicueta, Rüdiger, David Luiz, Emerson, Kante, Jorginho, Barkley (Loftus-Cheek), Pedro (Hudson-Odoi), Hazard, Willian (Higuain).

PENALTY shoot-outs are designed to make heroes out of keepers.

But Chelsea keeper Kepa ended up an anti-hero when defying his manager's furious touchline requests to come off in the final minutes of extra time after appearing to injure himself saving a shot from Aguero.

And that meant that our ex-keeper Willy Caballero became an innocent bystander in the car crash drama involving Chelsea boss

Maurizio Sarri and the aforementioned Kepa Arrizabalaga.

Willy, had of course, been the archetypal hero in City's League Cup win over Liverpool three years earlier.

But now, stripped off and ready for action, he could only wave his arms around and look puzzled and surprised as Kepa refused point blank to follow his manager's angry gestures.

All of which meant that Raheem Sterling's ice-cool penalty which settled the issue in favour of the Blues after what was an entertaining 0-0 stalemate over 120 minutes, was overshadowed.

The shoot-out itself was exciting enough without everything that had gone before it as extra-time drew to a close with the teams still deadlocked.

Ederson saved the first Chelsea effort from 12 yards – by Jorginho. Then Gundogan, Aguero and Bernardo netted for the Blues, while David Luiz struck a post.

And even though Sane's effort was saved by the Kepa, and Azplicueta, Emerson and Hazard all managed to score, it was Sterling who hammered the ball into the top right-hand corner of Arrizabalaga's goal for the decisive strike.

The Blues were several notches below their silky-smooth best, but they had to contend with a team smarting from the 6-0 beating they had given them at the Etihad two weeks earlier.

Sarri was determined that wouldn't happen again – and succeeded, but in doing so emasculated Chelsea's attacking threat with the result that they had only 31 per cent of possession and didn't produce a single shot on target in 90 minutes of normal time.

Bernardo tried his heart out – as he almost always does – and was a worthy winner of the Man of the Match accolade, but he couldn't quite set up the goal that might have been enough to win such a tight tussle. Of course, he concluded a typical shift at the coal face by doing the business from the spot.

It could have all finished much earlier – and no one would have been talking about Arrizabalaga's mutinous behaviour if Aguero's second-half goal hadn't been ruled out by VAR.

At the time it didn't look that close, but watching it again several times subsequently it was the proverbial width of a cigarette paper that denied our legendary all-time record goalscorer.

At the other end, Kante scooped one over the bar and Ederson did brilliantly to tip another Chelsea effort out of harm's way before Aguero went close again, just failing to connect cleanly after Sterling had pulled one back from the goal line.

And it was Aguero in the thick of it again in the dying embers of the extra 30 minutes when Sane took advantage of a slip by Rudiger to set up the Argentine, but once more he wasn't quite at his most decisive best with Arrizabalaga grabbing the shot at the second attempt.

The goalkeeper appeared to injure his hamstring for the second time and that's when all hell broke loose on the touchline.

KEPA SURVIVES, BUT SARRI DOESN'T Sarri's Chelsea tenure was over by the end of the season even though he won the Europa League, but Kepa Arrizabalaga survived him and although mainly out of favour recently he is still with the club at the time of writing and was an unused sub in Chelsea's Champions League win over the Blues in 2021. Arrizabalaga went from zero to hero in August 2021 when manager Thomas Tuchel brought him on in the penultimate minute of extra time, specifically to face a penalty shoot-out in the Super Cup Final against Villarreal in Belfast. Kepa did the job, saving two of the seven spot kicks he faced as the Stamford Bridge side won 6-5 on pens after a 1-1 draw in 120 minutes.

NOT CHEAP Arrizabalaga joined Chelsea from Athletic Bilbao for £71.6 million, making him the world's most expensive goalkeeper.

NO SMOKE WITHOUT FIRE Sarri is such a heavy smoker that in 2018, his Napoli team's Europa League opponents RB Leipzig built a special smoking section in the dressing room area of their stadium, the Red Bull Arena, specifically for him when the Italian team visited Leipzig. Sarri often chews cigarette butts on the touchline.

OFF TARGET This was the first League Cup final to end goalless since 2009, when Manchester United beat Spurs on penalties.

PEP TALK Here's what Guardiola said afterwards: "I'm happy. Chelsea did an incredible performance. In the penalties anything could happen and we're lucky. I'm happy to win back to back in this competition. I don't know if you realise the quality of the players Chelsea have."

DID YOU KNOW? There is actually an assistant video assistant referee! For this match Steve Child, of London, held that role, assisting the video assistant.

Chapter 34

THE ECSTASY AND THE AGONY

City 4 Tottenham Hotspur 3
Champions League Quarter-final Second leg
Etihad Stadium
Wednesday 17 April 2019
Attendance: 53,348

City: Ederson, Walker, Kompany, Laporte, Mendy (Sane), Gundogan, Silva (Fernandinho), De Bruyne, Bernardo, Sterling, Aguero. [**Sterling 2, Bernardo, Aguero**]

Manager: Pep Guardiola

Tottenham Hotspur: Lloris, Trippier, Alderweireld, Vertonghen, Rose (Sanchez), Wanyama, Sissoko (Llorente), Alli, Eriksen, Son, Moura (Davies). [**Son 2, Llorente**]

IN THE space of 65 seconds at the end of this absolutely classic encounter, City fans went from euphoria to despair as a night of high emotion unfolded at the Etihad.

When it looked as though Raheem Sterling had grabbed a sensational winner midway through the five minutes of added time, there were scenes of total mayhem in the stadium.

With the Spurs players lying on the pitch and their fans ready to walk away into the night, we were being told that the VAR was checking our "winner".

133

It happened as my son Edward and I were celebrating wildly, hugging complete strangers in the nearby seats. We were in the semi-finals of the Champions League. Or were we?

Edward pointed out – even in the midst of all the joyous scenes of delirium – that he had seen Bernardo looking across to the linesman on the far side from where we were sitting.

And then the unbelievable, unbearable news filtered through that Sterling's effort had been ruled out.

It was hard to describe how we felt; hard to describe how every City fan must have felt.

But the harsh, unpalatable truth was that we were out despite having probably turned in our best-ever European performance – and remember, we have beaten Champions League giants like Barcelona and Bayern Munich in the past (our home and away wins against Real Madrid and PSG wouldn't happen until the following Covid-ravaged seasons.)

We were out despite having turned around a 1-0 deficit from the first leg where Aguero had missed a penalty; out despite winning 4-3 on the night; out on away goals.

If the finish would never be forgotten for all the wrong reasons, how about the start, possibly the most amazing opening 20 minutes in the long and distinguished history of the competition.

Those first 20 minutes of the tie were frantic to say the least so here's a timeline of how it all happened to make it easier to understand:

3 mins 51 secs: City make a dream start when Sterling scores a beauty to make it 1-0 on the night and 1-1 on aggregate.

6 mins 52 secs: Our nemesis, Son Heung-min, who had netted the only goal in the first leg, equalises on the night to hand Spurs a 2-1 advantage overall.

9 mins 2 secs: Son does it again – and I must say Laporte wasn't at his best in either incident involving the South Korean – to give the North Londoners a 2-1 lead (3-1 on aggregate). If it was difficult before, it's daunting now.

10 mins 43 secs: Bernardo manages to get one past Lloris, thanks to a deflection. It might not have been going in, but who cares? We're now level on the night once again, but still trailing 3-2 in the tie.

20 mins 32 secs: A brilliant cross from man of the match De Bruyne is slammed past the Spurs keeper by Sterling. We're 3-2 ahead and level on aggregate.

I've watched a lot of football over the years, but I can't remember a more sensational start to a big game.

Truth be told, not much happened in the rest of the first half.

So, all we needed to do was win the second half...

And, almost as scripted, the legend that is Sergio Aguero scored a trademark goal to give us a 4-2 lead on the night in the 59th minute after De Bruyne had sliced open the Spurs defence, Sergio's howitzer of a shot almost going straight through Lloris.

The equation now was simple: Hold on for 31 minutes plus any added time and we're in the semi-final.

But the drama had only just begun.

Fernando Llorente, on as a first-half substitute for the injured Moussa Sissoko, bundled the ball home as Spurs reduced their deficit to 3-4.

VAR had a look and ruled that the goal stood, although replays I watched later suggested that the ball may have brushed Llorente's arm and come off his hip or thigh as it beat Ederson. Refereeing expert Peter Walton told BT Sport viewers the ball had clearly struck the Spaniard's knee!

But the goal stood and we still needed another goal.

Everyone in the stadium, including the Spurs players and supporters, thought we'd got that vital goal when Bernardo inadvertently put the ball into Aguero's path via a deflection and the Argentine's cross was converted by Sterling.

Cue pandemonium.

Sterling wheeled away in delight; the Spurs players lay on the turf, each like a boxer on the canvas after suffering a knockout blow at the end of a big fight.

The City fans in the crowd felt they had just witnessed one of the greatest victories in the club's history.

But once again the dreaded VAR machinery had the last word as just over a minute after Sterling had completed his hat-trick, the big screens at either end of the ground flashed up 'No goal – offside'.

It was only when I was researching for this book that I finally looked at the footage of those final few minutes. And, yes, under the laws of the game, Aguero was offside.

It was a long, silent drive home.

NO ATMOSPHERE? City fans have often been accused – sometimes unfairly – of not creating much of atmosphere, especially at the Etihad. But on this night, I don't think I've been at a match with such an extraordinary and tumultuous 'wall of sound' backdrop.

Not even wins over Man United or Liverpool or the epoch-making Aguerooo moment against QPR could better these noise levels.

It was a rare combination of dazzling attacking football and some suspect defending from the Blues allied to the fact that from start to finish no one in the crowd had a clue as to how it would all end. That's what made this game so special and Blues fans acknowledge it by giving the team a standing ovation at the end. You just had to have been there.

DID YOU KNOW? All five shots on target in the first half resulted in a goal.

WHAT THE BBC SAID: "Our thoughts go out to those that don't like football."

WHAT GUARDIOLA SAID: "It is cruel but it is what it is and we have to accept it. I am so proud of the players and the fans. I have never heard noise like that since I have been in Manchester but football is unpredictable.

"I support VAR but maybe from one angle Fernando Llorente's goal is handball, maybe from the referee's angle it is not."

PLAYING IT BY THE BOOK Despite the game's frantic pace, not a single City player was booked, while four Spurs players – Rose, Wanyama, Sissoko and Son – found their way into Turkish referee Cuneyt Cakir's notebook.

THREE DAYS LATER City and Spurs were in Etihad action again in the Premier League when a fifth minute goal from Phil Foden was the difference between the teams. City had to dig deep at times with two emotionally-drained sides – and two sets of emotionally-drained fans – slugging it out once more.

Chapter 35

KOMPANY'S CLASSIC

City 1 Leicester City 0
Premier League
Etihad Stadium
Monday 6 May 2019
Attendance: 54,506

City: Ederson, Walker, Kompany, Laporte, Zinchenko, Foden (Sane), Gundogan, D Silva (Stones), Bernardo, Aguero (Jesus), Sterling. [**Kompany**]

Manager: Pep Guardiola

Leicester City: Schmeichel, Pereira, Evans, Maguire, Chilwell, Albrighton (Gray), Tielemans (Barnes), Ndidi, Choudhury, Maddison (Iheanacho), Vardy.

'NO VINNY, don't shoot' – that was the plea from Sergio Aguero as skipper Vincent Kompany shaped to have a crack at goal from about 25 yards.

Of course, in those pre-Covid days, no one in the crowd had a clue that Aguero was imploring his captain to give the ball to someone else.

In Covid times, in empty stadiums up and down the land, the shouts of coaches and players could be heard ringing out, picked up by the TV companies' effects microphones dotted around the pitch.

This night at the Etihad, all one could hear was the growing frustration of the 50,000 City fans who had been trying desperately for 70 minutes to will their team to a victory that would put them within touching distance of retaining their Premier League crown.

Vinny heard all right, but he wasn't listening – either to the crowd or his team-mates.

Receiving the ball from Aymeric Laporte, Captain Kompany found himself in space as he strode towards the Leicester penalty area with a host of defenders backing off, clearly not expecting a shot.

After all, Kompany had not scored all season – and here we were in the final home game of the campaign.

And he claimed afterwards he had never ever scored from outside the penalty area in 15 years of top-flight football.

But the City skipper proved everyone wrong and, in the process, scored a goal that not only will he treasure for the rest of his mortal days, but a strike that gave his side a vital three points, leaving them the not-too-Herculean task of winning their final game of the season at Brighton to clinch back-to-back titles.

From my view, high in Colin Bell Level Two, I was almost in line with Kompany when he unleashed his match-winning thunderbolt, which gave our former keeper Kasper Schmeichel absolutely no chance as it arrowed into the top corner.

For most of this tense encounter, a winner hadn't looked like coming.

In fact, Leicester had looked the likelier team to grab a goal in the opening ten minutes when Kompany – staking an early claim for man of the match – was forced to block a fierce shot as the ball ricocheted around Ederson's goal like a pinball machine on amphetamines.

Finally, the danger was cleared – and gradually City got on top with several close calls for the Foxes' defence.

Aguero was twice in range without hitting the target, with a header striking the bar and another effort being stopped by Schmeichel's outstretched leg. There were several other good efforts from the

Blues forwards and midfielders, but it was centre-back Kompany who rode to the rescue.

Ten minutes after his goal, Leicester introduced another of our former players, Kelechi Iheanacho, who may well have had a point to prove against his old team.

And he had the chance to do just that with only a few minutes left on the clock, finding himself put through on goal. But he rushed the shot, which looked easier on the night than it did watching it again some months later, and the ball went wide with Ederson scrambling along his line.

There were no further alarms and the points were duly pocketed. Three more and the title would be ours again no matter what second-placed Liverpool might do in their final game.

Kompany and the rest of his team-mates paraded round the Etihad – some with their children in tow – as the team thanked the fans for their support.

The captain shed more than a tear or two as he led the side round with his four kids wearing City kits.

No one knew at the time, although many had guessed, that this was to be his last home game in a City kit himself.

He played 86 minutes at Brighton the following Sunday as City clinched the title and all 90 minutes at Wembley on May 18 in the 6-0 FA Cup Final rout of Watford before announcing his departure from the club the following day.

What a fantastic final 12 days. What a fantastic City career.

WHAT THEY SAID Vincent Kompany: "Don't shoot, don't shoot. I could really hear it; it was annoying me and I thought 'hold on a second I have not come this far in my career for young players to tell me when I can take a shot or not'. I just took it.

"All I can say is that I've scored goals in training like that for 15 years. But I haven't scored one like that (from outside the penalty area) in 15 years of top-level football.

"You know what, it's a funny story. It's 15 years of having midfielders tell me, 'Don't shoot! Play the ball wide!' For 15 years I've said, 'One day I'm going to have a shot from outside the box, and it's going to go in, and you're going to be happy with that one'."

THINKING OUTSIDE THE BOX Although Kompany claimed in his post-match interview that he hadn't scored from outside the box in 15 years, it is believed he netted one such goal for Hamburg against Brann in an away UEFA Cup tie in October 2007 – only 11 years earlier. Like tonight, it was the only goal of the game.

WHAT THEY SAID Pep Guardiola: "One game left, and it will be so tough like today. We are away and we saw Brighton had a good game at Arsenal. But it is in our hands, don't forget but we could have been 10 points behind if we lost to Liverpool here.

"We were seven points behind, but we are in the last game and it is in our hands. We are going to prepare well.

"We'll see if Brighton defend deep or will be more offensive. It will be tough, but hopefully we will have the performance to be champions."

DID YOU KNOW? The BBC website voted Kasper Schmeichel man of the match.

LUCKY CHARM? Mike Dean, referee on the evening, took charge of City's defeat at the King Power Stadium earlier in the season in December, but since then had officiated two Blues' games, resulting in 9-0 and 6-0 wins. Dean was, of course, in charge of City's famous 3-2 win over QPR in 2012.

DID YOU KNOW? The lead at the top of the table changed hands no fewer than 32 times during the Premier League season.

Chapter 36

THE FRIENDLY FINAL

City 6 Watford 0
Wembley Stadium
FA Cup Final
Saturday 18 May 2019
Attendance: 85,854

City: Ederson, Walker, Kompany, Laporte, Zinchenko, Bernardo Silva, Gundogan (Sane), David Silva (Stones), Mahrez (De Bruyne), Jesus, Sterling. [**David Silva, Sterling 2, De Bruyne, Jesus 2**]

Manager: Pep Guardiola

Watford: Gomes; Femenia, Mariappa, Cathcart, Holebas, Hughes, (Cleverley) Capoue, Doucoure, Pereyra (Success); Deulofeu (Gray) Deeney.

IT WAS dubbed the Friendly Final as Watford rolled over to have their tummies tickled by the silky-smooth Blue machine.

I nearly said well-oiled machine, but that would have only added fuel to the already-smouldering fire and generated even more abusive comments from the keyboard warriors about how City were "killing the game".

At the time, I'm sure I wasn't the only Blues fan feeling a little – only a little – sorry for Watford as they were taken apart piece by piece.

But doing some research for this chapter on the BBC website, I checked out many of the 2,299 comments posted during and after the match.

The overwhelming majority had absolutely no hesitation in banging on about a mis-match that had come about as a result of our super-wealthy owners; owners who were ruining the game.

There were a few from what appear to be City fans – we didn't need to comment really, I think our performance spoke for itself – but the vast majority were fairly obviously either Liverpool or Man United fans, the majority of whom, I would hazard a guess, hadn't set foot in either Anfield or Old Trafford, and that was before Covid padlocked all grounds.

Here are some typical ones: *Well done, Watford. The only difference between the two clubs... Sheikh Mansour and creative accountancy...*

Gulf oil money wins again

When UEFA find Man City guilty of Financial Fair Play Regulations, will they be disqualified from the trophies they won, seeing as they won them by cheating. I'm going to have a wild guess that they'll pay their way out of that one as well...

Congrats to Abu Dhabi football club on cheating their way to another undeserved trophy. Remember:

Roses are Red...
Violets are Blue...
If it wasn't for oil...
You would be in League 2...

Poetic licence, I suppose.

But a few posters hit back *Enjoy it city fans you lot dropped down the leagues and still packed our away end. Sod the jealous fans and enjoy it while you can – Wolves fan.*

And another: *Crikey! The level of envy on here is ridiculous! Great performance, great season, all top 6 teams got financial support on level with City but not got the management to deal with it. Fully deserved and congrats to Man City! Well done Watford and respect to their supporters! Pure class!*

And here's one more from another neutral: *While you're all on here rotten to the core with resentment and jealousy (oh YES you REALLY are) City fans are out on the town celebrating the treble. Do talk amongst yourselves. Not a City supporter either – Just a grown up.*

Watford, of course, were massive underdogs. There were 48 points between the teams in the Premier League – and it showed.

Yes, football's a funny old game, but not that funny. Well, not very often.

Actually, Watford started really well and Roberto Pereyra missed an early chance to put his side ahead – denied by a good save by Ederson's right-foot as the Brazilian stopper rushed off his line.

Ederson did the right thing. There were no City defenders within striking distance of Pereyra after he was put in the clear by a swift Hornets' move after Zinchenko had lost the ball in a crucial midfield area. But the chance – a rare one for the Hertfordshire side – came and went.

Not long afterwards there was an appeal for handball against Kompany, who was turning away as a shot hit him on the arm inside the area. No dice said referee Kevin Friend.

Then the blue tide turned inexorably against Watford and, in the end, City were clear winners on the field, with Watford's fan base clear winners off it.

The Hornets' supporters simply didn't stop cheering their side – and towards the closing stages, the City fans acknowledged Watford's unwavering support; support which stayed behind after the final whistle to celebrate 'just being there'.

So, unlike the fans of the so-called big sides who have been beaten in a Wembley final who are usually on their way home long before the winners take the first steps up to the royal box, often not even waiting to acknowledge the efforts of their own team.

The first breach in the Watford defence came courtesy of 'Merlin', aka Spanish Dave, as silky Silva ended a scoring drought that had lasted for four months, latching on to a lovely pass from namesake,

Bernardo, to sweep the ball past Heurelho Gomes. **1-0**.

Jesus got in behind the Watford defence to double the advantage before half time, with Sterling following up to make sure it was over the line – he wasn't needed, the goal was given to the Brazilian. **2-0**.

After another sweeping move, came a truly astonishing piece of skill from De Bruyne as he shimmied this way and that way before drilling the ball into the corner after City cut through the Watford defence like a hot knife through Lurpak. **3-0**.

Jesus doubled his tally about seven minutes later, blasting the ball home to the delight of the City fans packed behind the goal. His trademark 'home' gesture said it all. **4-0**.

In the final ten minutes, great work by Bernardo set up Sterling for his first as he tricked Gomes before putting the ball underneath the keeper's body. **5-0**.

Before Sterling grabbed his second to round off a sensational afternoon, following up his own shot, which had struck the post and getting there first to beat the despairing dive of Gomes. **6-0**.

City captain Vincent Kompany probably summed it up best: "It wasn't as easy as the score makes it look. But what a season, what a tremendous club.

"It started with the manager; he sets the standard at the start of the season. It's the best team in the world for me."

Amen to that!

DID YOU KNOW? Kevin De Bruyne played for only 38 minutes, including second-half stoppage time – and still won Man of the Match! Almost certainly a record that will never be broken...

FIFTY UP City became the first English top-flight side to register 50 wins in all competitions in a single season.

SIX-SHOOTERS City became only the third team to score six goals in an FA Cup final, after Blackburn against Sheffield Wednesday in 1890 (6-1) and Bury against Derby in 1903 (6-0). So, finally, the Shakers record has been equalled.

Chapter 37

CITY GET REAL AT LAST

Real Madrid 1 City 2
Santiago Bernabéu Stadium
Champions League Round of 16
Wednesday 26 February 2020
Attendance: 75,615

Real Madrid: Courtois: Carvajal, Varane, Ramos, Mendy; Modrić (Lucas Vázquez), Casemiro, Valverde; Isco (Jović), Benzema, Vinícius Júnior (Bale). [**Isco**]

City: Ederson; Walker, Otamendi, Laporte (Fernandinho), Mendy; Gündoğan, Rodri, De Bruyne; Mahrez, Jesus, Bernardo (Sterling). [**Jesus**, **De Bruyne** pen]

Manager: Pep Guardiola

FROM my seat at the back of the fourth tier (of five), it all seemed so un-Real, if you'll pardon the pun and I think I'm allowed one pun at least to celebrate the club's first-ever win in six attempts against the Spanish behemoths – the team with the most wins in the history of the Champions League.

Earlier in the month we had been banned from Europe for two years by UEFA and we were all determined to enjoy what might have been our last European away trip for at least two campaigns.

But I was extremely nervous making the trip with the Covid-19 pandemic kicking off with a vengeance in Spain just about the same time as the teams were kicking off here.

Television pictures of ambulances and mortuaries from Spain's biggest cities did nothing to calm the nerves and it turned out that this was the last big game played on the Iberian Peninsula prior to the country locking down.

However, once the game began, everyone in the stadium was clearly focused – despite the wire mesh fencing that separated us from the home fans – on the prospect of 90 minutes of Champions League football in one of the world's most iconic stadiums.

And we might well have got off to a dream start on 20 minutes if Jesus had not been denied by a great save from Courtois. Then another effort from the City striker, although going wide, was diverted towards goal by one Real defender, only to be kicked off the line by another.

At the other end Ederson was called into action to make a fantastic save, but he couldn't hold onto the ball which was hacked away to safety.

It all went wrong on the hour mark when Otamendi, Rodri and Walker got themselves in a terrible muddle and Vinicius Junior took full advantage of the defensive lapse before squaring across goal for Isco to slot home past an angry Ederson.

A great block by Fernandinho prevented further damage soon afterwards and although we were looking the better side, it wasn't until 12 minutes from time that the breakthrough came our way.

Brilliant work by De Bruyne, who despite being surrounded by white shirts, managed to find the head of Jesus with one of his laser-guided crosses. The Brazilian got above Ramos and placed it past the former Chelsea keeper to make it 1-1.

There was, of course, a VAR check as the Madrid players claimed Jesus had pushed the Madrid centre-back, but the goal stood – and so did we!

Sterling had been introduced off the bench on 73 minutes and was causing all sorts of the problems for the Madrid defence. It was from one of his runs into the area that he won a penalty when he was brought down by a clumsy challenge from Carvajal. Ice-cool Kevin, showing no outward signs of the pressure he must surely have been under, slotted home from the spot.

That wasn't the end of the drama though. Jesus was sent clear and was bearing down on goal when Ramos brought him down just outside the box with a red card the inevitable result. From the resultant free-kick, Mahrez got past the wall, but couldn't beat Courtois.

Great result. Great occasion. Terrible view...

REAL CLASS Real Madrid have won the Champions League a staggering 13 times, almost twice as many successes as AC Milan, who have been crowned the top club side in Europe on seven occasions.

LONG WAIT Because of the Covid-19 pandemic, City would have to wait more than five months before playing the second leg behind closed doors at the Etihad.

PEP'S BOLD CALL Guardiola left Sterling, Aguero, Silva and Fernandinho on the bench, deploying Bernardo and De Bruyne as alternating false nines. Fernandinho replaced the injured Laporte after 33 minutes, while Sterling came on for Bernardo midway through the second half.

A VERY NAUGHTY BOY Sergio Ramos received his 26th red card as a Real Madrid player, four of them in the Champions League. But he's going to have to go some to claim a world red card record. That dubious honour belongs to Colombian enforcer Gerardo Bedoya, who was dismissed 46 times in a 20-year career with 12 different clubs in his homeland, Argentina and Mexico. The Colombian international certainly earned the nickname of "The Beast".

RECORD BREAKER City's win was Guardiola's 28th in the CL knockout stages – more than any other manager in the competition's history.

WHAT GUARDIOLA SAID: "When we were better, we conceded a goal. When they were better, we scored a goal. That's football. I remember the quarter-final [against Liverpool] a few seasons ago at Anfield when we played incredibly well and they scored (with) all their shots on target."

UEFA VERDICT UEFA technical director Roberto Martinez, who awarded De Bruyne the man of the match accolade, said of the Belgian: "He was at the centre of every attacking threat for City. His clever positioning on the ball allowed City to create numerical advantages all over the pitch."

HOME VIEW Real Madrid reporter Graham Hunter said: "Since November, Madrid have bristled with energy, wave after wave of pressing attacks, and the feeling they have 12 men on the pitch. What horrid timing that just as the business end of the season arrives, in knockout form, they've dipped in terms of sharpness and stamina." Not a lot of credit for City there then.

AWAY VIEW City reporter Simon Hart said: "Guardiola opted for an unfamiliar strategy with De Bruyne and Bernardo Silva attacking centrally from deep and Jesus stationed out wide. He had used something similar in City's January League Cup semi-final win at Manchester United and it paid off again here with a goal from Jesus – vindicating his surprise selection ahead of Sergio Agüero – before the fresh legs of substitute Sterling won their match-winning penalty. Credit too for the way they recovered from the loss of Aymeric Laporte to injury and concession of an avoidable opener."

Chapter 38

THE MODERN HOLY TRINITY

City 2 Aston Villa 1
Wembley Stadium
Carabao Cup Final
Sunday 1 March 2020
Attendance: 82,145

City: Bravo, Walker, Stones, Fernandinho, Zinchenko, Gundogan (De Bruyne), Rodri, Foden, Silva (Bernardo), Sterling, Aguero (Jesus). **[Aguero, Rodri]**

Manager: Pep Guardiola

Aston Villa: Nyland, Guilbert, Engels, Mings, Targett, Luiz, Nakamba, Elmohamady (Hourihane), Grealish, El Ghazi (Trezeguet), Samatta (Davis). **[Samatta]**

I GREW up in the Bell-Lee-Summerbee era, but how about this for a Holy Trinity: Fernandinho-Aguero-Silva.

The latter threesome has had phenomenal success in Sky Blue shirts and their League Cup record may never be surpassed.

This victory over Villa gave them a remarkable fifth triumph offering stability in a competition that has been played under the names of multiple different sponsors (see below).

But these three City names will be etched into the tournament's history forever.

The trio first got together in the Blues 2014 triumph and were there for the Wembley wins in 2016, 2018, 2019 and this one in 2020.

Of course, City made it four in a row and six in eight years against Spurs the following year when Aguero was an unused substitute (see Chapter 45). Here, the evergreen Fernandinho was the only "survivor".

However, despite our wealth of experience on the big stage, it wasn't quite the cruise to victory that recent form and the bookmakers' odds had suggested.

We had thumped relegation-threatened Villa 6-1 in our most recent meeting and were coming into the game after a superb Champions League win at Real Madrid in midweek. Unsurprisingly, the Midlanders were somewhere around 14-1 to produce one of the biggest upsets in the competition's history.

But they almost drew first blood, missing a good opportunity in only the third minute when Anwar El Ghazi's header landed on top of the netting.

Normal service was resumed, however, in the 20th minute when one of our Three League Cup musketeers – Aguero – grabbed the first goal of the contest after a slick move involving Sterling, Rodri and Foden, who cushioned a neat header into Sergio's path with the latter doing what he does best to make it 1-0.

Foden was in the thick of the action soon afterwards when sending the ball flashing across the face of goal after stylishly bringing Zinchenko's pass under control.

Then came a disputed corner kick from which Gundogan found the head of Rodri, who powered the ball past Nyland – and that was 2-0.

Game over? Not really.

We could have actually gone further ahead when a Sterling shot was blocked by Tyrone Ming's upper arm, but on 41 minutes, Villa pulled one back.

John Stones misjudged a flighted ball from just inside the City half and fell as he did so, compounding the error. From the resultant cross, Mbwana Samatta beat Bravo comprehensively with a brilliant, flying header.

So, instead of going in at the interval three or four goals to the good, we went in with only a one-goal lead.

There were three fairly decent chances to build on that lead in the second period, but it was Villa who came closest with two minutes left of the 90 when Bravo pushed a Bjorn Engels' header against the post and Stones, making up for his earlier lapse in concentration and balance, hacked the ball to safety.

SUPER PERFORMANCE The *Independent's* Miguel Delaney, who has never been known to miss an opportunity to point out of how much we have spent, as well as noting that the Blues had won six of the last seven domestic trophies, wrote: "That is some level of success, that reflects the machine that this super-powered super-funded club has become. It has brought a super level of talent, from the intelligence of manager Pep Guardiola, to the stellar ability of goalscorer Sergio Aguero, and the sprightly quality of homegrown Phil Foden."

HARD CURRENCY The *Guardian's* David Hytner said: "Manchester City had no time for the romance of Aston Villa's Carabao Cup final story. Pep Guardiola and his players deal only in the hard currency of domestic trophies and they extended their grip on it via a performance of near suffocating control."

UNLUCKY VILLA? The corner that brought City's second goal was hotly disputed by Villa – and their fans massed behind the goal where the incident occurred were quick to show their displeasure. To be fair, it appeared to come off Gundogan rather than Grealish, so there were grounds for complaints, but whether it was a harsh decision or not, Villa failed to defend the corner properly. On the run of play, though, Dean Smith's side could have few complaints about the result.

DROUGHT CONTINUES Villa's wait for a trophy continues. They hadn't won silverware since Brian Little led them to a League Cup triumph in 1996.

WEMBLEY WONDERS It was City's eighth successive victory across all competitions at the national stadium, a run that stretches back to our Carabao Cup Final win in 2018.

WHAT'S IN A NAME? The League Cup has had more name changes than any other domestic English competition. It started life as the Football League Cup in 1960-61 when Villa were the inaugural winners, and remained under this guise until 1980-81, with the competition having no main title sponsor in its first 20 years. The first sponsors were the Milk Marketing Board with the competition rebranded as the Milk Cup. Subsequent names: Littlewoods Challenge Cup, Rumbelows Cup, Coca-Cola Cup, Worthington Cup, Carling Cup, Capital One Cup, EFL Cup (when it had no major sponsor for the 2016-17 season) and, finally, the Carabao Cup from 2017-18 to the present day.

Chapter 39

A PIECE OF CAKE (AND A CUP OF TEA) FOR THE BLUES

City 4 Liverpool 0
Etihad Stadium
Premier League
Thursday 2 July 2020
Attendance: Nil

City: Ederson, Walker (Cancelo), Garcia, Laporte (Otamendi), Mendy, Gundogan, Rodri, Foden, De Bruyne, Sterling, (Bernardo), Jesus (Mahrez). [**De Bruyne** pen, **Sterling, Foden, Oxlade-Chamberlain** og]

Manager: Pep Guardiola

Liverpool: Alisson, Alexander-Arnold (Williams), Gomez (Oxlade-Chamberlain), van Dijk, Robertson, Henderson, Fabinho, Wijnaldum (Keita), Salah, Firmino (Origi), Mane (Minamino).

CITY gave the newly-crowned champions a rather perfunctory guard of honour – and then a rather comprehensive beating.

But despite the margin of victory against the runaway leaders, it was the guard of honour that provided almost as many talking points in the post-match conversation.

It was the night Bernardo became Brewnardo! The Portuguese

playmaker, along, it must be said, with most of his colleagues wasn't ecstatic about having to line up and applaud the Liverpool team as it took to the field. So he didn't.

Bernardo, sorry Brewnardo, arrived to the party late, wearing an unfastened jacket over his training top and carrying a plastic cup of tea.

He barely glanced at the Liverpool players as they walked out behind their captain Jordan Henderson and was strolling, still carrying his pre-match brew, before many of the Merseysiders had made it past him.

He was revered and reviled on social media – and it wouldn't be too difficult to work out which team's fans were doing the revering and which the reviling.

Suffice to say, Bernardo became some sort of Etihad folk hero that evening.

Once hostilities switched to the field, and remember, Bernardo didn't join in until the 79th minute when he replaced Raheem Sterling, it was a comfortable night for the Blues once they had weathered a typical early Liverpool storm.

That spell of bad weather for City's defence peaked when Salah struck the post with Ederson beaten, but Mane couldn't control the rebound and although they had one or two other opportunities in the first half of the first half, in truth, Klopp's 'mentality monsters' were not quite at it.

And by the 25th minute the visitors were behind when Joe Gomez became so attracted to Sterling in the Liverpool penalty area that he wouldn't let go of the former Anfield favourite.

Of course, Sterling and Gomez have "history". The former notably squared up to the latter during an England training session on the day after Sterling felt he had been subjected to some rough treatment by Gomez at Anfield 24 hours earlier.

That time, the "referee" was England boss Gareth Southgate, who promptly dropped Sterling from the side for the game against Montenegro; Gomez came on as a sub for the last 20 minutes.

This time, the referee was Wythenshawe-born Anthony Taylor who had no hesitation in pointing to the spot and Kevin De Bruyne did the necessary, sending Alisson the wrong way.

Some great play led to Foden setting up Sterling and although the shot wasn't the best, it was enough to get it over the line. Sterling's first Premier League goal against his old club on his ninth attempt.

Foden, having one of those nights when he looks every inch a generational talent, made it 3-0 in the 35th minute and Alex Oxlade-Chamberlain rounded it all off by deflecting a Sterling shot that was going wide past his own keeper on 66 minutes.

Quite a contribution from the former Southampton and Arsenal man who had only been on since half time after replacing Gomez, who had endured a torrid time trying to tame Sterling.

There would have been a fifth, but for the intervention of the VAR after Mahrez had beaten the Liverpool keeper at his near post, but Foden was adjudged to have handled the ball in the build-up. It mattered not a jot.

CAUGHT OFF GUARD City's pre-match welcome to the side that had taken their title might have been a little lukewarm, but in the following season, Celtic refused point blank to applaud their bitter rivals, Rangers, onto the field at Parkhead after Steven Gerrard's team had won their first Scottish title in a decade. Stand-in manager John Kennedy, appointed after Neil Lennon (who actually made one first team appearance for City) resigned, said: "We've spoken collectively about it and won't do it." Fair enough, then.

DID YOU KNOW? Despite suffering just their second league loss of the campaign, clinching the title with seven games to go is the earliest any team in English top-flight history has managed to achieve the feat.

WHAT THE MANAGERS SAID Guardiola: "I'm delighted. Congratulations to the team, we beat the champions with the quality they have. I saw in the guard of honour how incredibly focused they (Liverpool) were, how they shouted. I saw their faces, that's why they're champions." **Klopp:** "Is the game important to us? I saw a brilliant attitude. They were quicker than us in mind. We lacked fluidity."

NOT-SO-HAPPY HUNTING GROUND Liverpool's two heaviest Premier League defeats under Klopp have both been at the Etihad Stadium against City (4-0 in this game and 5-0 in September 2017).

HANGOVER: This was the joint-heaviest defeat by a side already crowned Premier League champions in a season, with Arsenal losing 4-0 away at Liverpool in 1997-98, which was also the game after they won the title.

Chapter 40

A FITTING TRIBUTE TO THE KING

Manchester United 0 City 2
Old Trafford
Carabao Cup Semi-final
Wednesday, 6 January 2021
Attendance: Nil

City: Steffen, Cancelo, Stones, Dias, Zinchenko, De Bruyne, Fernandinho, Gundogan, Sterling, Mahrez [Rodri], Foden. [**Stones, Fernandinho**]

Manager: Pep Guardiola

Manchester United: Henderson, Wan-Bissaka, Lindelof, Maguire, Shaw, Fred (Van de Beek), McTominay (Greenwood), Rashford, Fernandes, Pogba, Martial

---

COLIN BELL was my inspiration growing up. He was about my age, but while I was churning out cliché-crammed reports on amateur football for a local paper, he was playing for City and England.

He was, without doubt, the greatest City footballer of his era, although my Dad always insisted Peter Doherty was better.

Subsequently, only perhaps David Silva and Kevin De Bruyne could have been spoken of in the same breath as the King of the Kippax, but Bell started it all for me.

So, it was fitting that on the day after Bell's death, City dedicated this win over United to the man they dubbed Nijinsky.

They had entered the Old Trafford pitch wearing vintage pale blue City shirts all bearing Bell's No. 8 on the back.

If they had kept them on over the ensuing 90 minutes, I don't think Ole Gunnar Solksjaer's team could have been less confused.

As it was, this was as comfortable a victory as it gets over the red half of the city.

Some years earlier in this very competition, Guardiola had maybe misjudged the animosity between the fans of the two sides when putting out a strangely under-strength team in the fourth round in October 2016 when Pep made nine changes while United's then manager Jose Mourinho opted to field a full-strength side including Zlatan Ibrahimovic, Paul Pogba and Marcus Rashford, with Ibrahimovic grabbing the winner in the 55th minute. It remains, at the time of writing, the last time we were knocked out of the competition although we did suffer a second leg 1-0 defeat to the Stretford side at the Etihad a year earlier, going through 3-2 on aggregate after a 3-1 win in the first leg.

Knowing, as we do, that Pep understands more about Manchester's footballing history than most fans, possibly he felt that his selected team would do the business anyway.

Conceivably, it was a case of "over-thinking", something he has occasionally been accused of indulging in – you only have to look back to the 3-1 Champions League quarter-final defeat by a fairly average Lyon team in a tie that was switched to Lisbon in 2020 because of the Covid-19 pandemic.

But Guardiola, who wore a 'Bell Legend' T-shirt, was totally aware of Bell's legendary status – and just how much he meant to City fans, and not just those of a certain age. So, the line-up was probably the strongest team he could have fielded on the night, with US international Zack Steffen deputising for the Brazilian in goal, as is customary under Pep in Carabao and FA Cup ties.

After the dismantling of Chelsea the previous weekend, this was further proof that City were firmly back on the right road.

Bell himself would have relished the way City went about the task of booking their fourth successive Carabao Cup Final date at Wembley, having, of course, won their previous three.

In truth there wasn't much between the two sides at half time, with three "goals" disallowed for offside in the first 24 minutes – all correctly I believe – and a De Bruyne shot hitting the post with keeper Dean Henderson a spectator.

Come the second half and it was John Stones, enjoying a renaissance at centre-back, where he has been paired with the immaculate Ruben Dias, who popped up to score his first City goal for 1,162 days.

The goal certainly wasn't a classic. It appeared to come off his thigh or some other part of his nether regions – but who cares. Every goal against United should be considered a classic. Well, that's my view.

It began with a free kick taken by Foden and Stones, lurking in the "corridor of uncertainty" between Luke Shaw and Harry Maguire, managed to persuade the ball into the back of the net.

From that point on, City controlled matters with the Dias-Stones axis so important at the back, giving Anthony Martial and Marcus Rashford precious few opportunities, and Fernandinho running the show in midfield. Bruno Fernandes did draw a good save from Steffen, but that was about as good as it got for the home side, who were without the suspended Edinson Cavani.

Fittingly, it was Ferna who made the game safe seven minutes from time when Aaron Wan-Bissaka nodded an attempted clearance straight to him and he volleyed low inside Henderson's right-hand post.

Afterwards, Stones told the media: "We dedicate this win to Colin Bell and his family. How we played in this match was a reflection of him. It was a great moment and I'm sure he was looking down on us."

BELL'S NICKNAME Apart from King of the Kippax Bell was also affectionately known to Blues fans as Nijinsky after the racehorse for his combination of speed and stamina. Nijinsky, the horse, was one of the greatest of all time, winning the Triple Crown – all three Classics, the 2,000 Guineas at Newmarket, the Derby at Epsom and the St Leger at Doncaster in 1970. Many experts believe he was the best European Flat horse of the twentieth century.

KING OF THE FANZINES *King of the Kippax*, City's only surviving fanzine, is named after the incomparable Colin Bell's nickname. It's always worth buying. I should know, I write for them every month!

PEP'S MOJO A Sky Sports interviewer told Pep: "It looks like you've got your mojo back. "Who?" he queried. The interviewer replied: "You've got your magic back; that Manchester City feel again."

POSITIVE RESULTS Eight City players had tested positive for Covid-19 in the 14 days prior to the match.

DID YOU KNOW? This was United's fourth successive semi-final defeat.

Chapter 41

JAB AND MOVE

City 4 Crystal Palace 0
Etihad Stadium
Premier League
Sunday, 17 January 2021
Attendance: Nil

City: Ederson, Walker, Stones, Dias, De Bruyne (Cancelo), Fernandinho, Gundogan (Torres), Zinchenko, Bernardo (Foden), Jesus, Sterling. [**Stones** 2**, Gundogan, Sterling**]

Manager: Pep Guardiola

Crystal Palace: Guaita, Mitchell, Cahill, Tomkins, Ward, Milivojevic (Riedewald), Eze, McArthur, Townsend (Batshuayi), Ayew.

WE ARE in the middle of the biggest health crisis of the century – the Covid-19 pandemic that cost millions of lives across the planet.

One of the few remaining pleasures is watching Premier League football on the box.

Tonight's offering is against a Palace side, missing their one proper, star player, Wilfried Zaha, who had been injured in their previous match.

But after asking the local pharmacist – almost in desperation – whether there might be any 'spares' of the vaccine for myself and the wife, I'm half-listening out for the familiar ring of my mobile phone as the match gets underway.

The pharmacy owner, a good friend of ours, had said earlier in the week that he'd put us both on his 'waiting list'. I'm sure we're entitled to be on the list: we're in the right age category and qualify as CEVs – Clinically Extremely Vulnerable for the uninitiated.

For four days, though, he hasn't got back to me. Hassan, of course, is mad busy – and he's a United fan so maybe it was all a cruel joke.

Hassan was one of the first pharmacists in the UK to hand out the life-saving vaccinations. His shop was mentioned in a press release sent out by Whitehall and he even got a visit from the vaccine minister Nadhim Zahawi in a photo opportunity on the day he started putting jabs into arms.

I'm still half-staring at the silent mobile when John Stones scores his first-ever Premier League goal for the club from a beautiful cross from De Bruyne, almost caressed with the outside of his right foot, with the ball making a delicious arc on its way to Stones' head.

The born-again centre-back, restored to the team and in the midst of a marvellous partnership with Dias, had netted his first City goal two-and-a-half weeks earlier when grabbing the first against United in a 2-0 Carabao Cup semi-final success.

That was, truth to tell, a bit of a scruffy effort – although every Blue goal is a good one, and doubly so against Ole Gunnar Solksjaer's team.

This KDB cross deserved a great finish – like a symphony needs a great final movement.

And Stones provided it, make no mistake about that.

We're 26 minutes in and one-up.

Still, the phone hasn't rung. A friend told me that 'spares' usually came on stream about 8pm. It's 7.41. We've still got time. There's still a chance.

Seven minutes later, my mobile lights up. It's Hassan: "It's your lucky day," he almost shouts down the line. "Get down here as quickly as you can, we've got vaccine for you and your wife!"

So, 34 minutes in, I'm hitting the pause button on the TV. A few minutes later, we're in the car on our way to the chemist.

Ten minutes after our breathless arrival, we're on our way back home, with some the finest Astra Zeneca-Oxford vaccine in our arms.

Jab and move, I told my better half. We got back as quickly as we got there.

Once home, I put the telly back on to catch up with the action. The half time interval enabled me to almost overtake the game itself and I'm watching it unfold live from quite early in the second half.

Good job, too, as Gundogan scores a screamer for our second, then Stones scores his second after his defensive partner Dias' header is pushed out by the Palace keeper Vicente Guaita and he follows up in the style of a regular goalscorer.

Sterling rounds off a great evening with our fourth from a well-placed free-kick that gave the Palace keeper no chance.

Game well and truly over and another three points pouched. The wife's smiling now she's had the jab and I'm beaming for two obvious reasons.

After this fifth consecutive PL win, City moved into second place (with a game in hand), two points off the summit – a far cry from being in 13th place after Spurs hit-and-run 2-0 win at the Tottenham Hotspur Stadium in November.

How's that for a great Sunday night!

STONES ME John Stones' two goals were his first successful strikes in the Premier League since he scored for Everton in April 2015. Surprisingly, this was the third double of Stones' senior career. He scored twice for the Blues against Feyenoord in September 2017 and doubled up for England against Panama at the 2018 World Cup.

TON UP Kevin De Bruyne's sublime pass for the first goal was his 100th assist in all competitions since joining the club in 2015 – that's 32 more than any other Premier League player since the Belgian made his debut for the Blues.

QUIET BIRTHDAY Pep celebrated his 50th birthday the next day – alone. His wife and family are back in Barcelona. "Now I will drink a good glass of wine and then think about Aston Villa (City's next fixture)," said the boss. If he stuck to one glass, I'm sure he would have raised it to the memory of his late mother, 82-year-old Dolors Sala Carrió, who succumbed from coronavirus in the early days of the pandemic. Soon afterwards, Pep donated one million euros to Spain's battle against the disease.

NOBEL PRIZE-WINNER? That should definitely go to whoever invented Sky Plus and the pause button! What on earth would we do without it?

Chapter 42

ABOUT TIME TOO

Liverpool 1 City 4
Anfield
Premier League
Sunday 7 February 2021
Attendance: Nil

Liverpool: Allison, Alexander-Armstrong, Fabinho, Henderson, Robertson (Tsimikas), Thiago Alcantara (Shaqiri), Wijnaldum, Jones (Milner), Salah, Firmino, Mane. [**Salah** pen]

City: Ederson, Cancelo, Stones, Dias, Zinchenko, Bernardo, Rodri, Gundogan, Mahrez (Jesus), Foden, Sterling. [**Gundogan 2, Sterling, Foden**]

Manager: Pep Guardiola

IT WAS City's first away win against Liverpool for 18 years. I wasn't present for this one and neither was anyone else and I wasn't there for the last one when Nicolas Anelka scored both goals, including a penalty deep into stoppage time, to give the Blues a 2-1 win against the side he had made 20 appearances for when on loan the previous season.

I had seen City lose multiple times at Anfield, one of the most painful being the 3-0 thrashing in 2011 when Andy Carroll – still playing apparently – scored twice in the first half. I'm not sure he's scored twice in a game since. Or even once!

But this time there was no Big Andy in the home ranks, only Salah, Mane and Firmino up front to worry us.

Worry us they didn't, once we got over a decent spell of Kloppball in the first half.

And we also shrugged off a missed penalty that would have given us a lead going into the interval. Gundogan was the culprit after Fabinho had fouled Sterling.

The latter, appearing in front of Anfield's wide-open, empty spaces and without the spiteful background noise the crowd here always reserves for their former player who they consider a "turncoat/ traitor" (take your pick), seemed to perform with a lot more freedom.

But even though Sterling did well, it was Foden who stole the show in a consummately skilful performance that showed that Pep had got it spot on in holding the youngster back before releasing him, fully formed as it were, on unsuspecting Premier League and European defences.

No one had ever doubted that the local lad – some call him the 'Stockport Iniesta' although I doubt the Barcelona star was as good as Foden may become.

Just like Guardiola has given young Phil a helping hand throughout his City career, the Blues were given an even bigger helping hand by Liverpool's Allison, who had a night to forget that Blues fans will long remember.

I suppose if you're going to have a bad night, you might as well have a really bad one; get it all out of your system.

Well, the Brazilian, a national teammate of our very own Ederson, who played four times at the Copa America finals, eventually ousting the Liverpool stopper from the side, made crucial errors at 1-1 that handed the advantage to the Blues.

Gundogan made up for his spot-kick blunder by putting City ahead just after half time when Allison made a really good stop from a Foden shot, but the ball travelled straight to the German who was delighted to make up for his penalty error.

But the game swung the other way when Salah showed the German how to do it from 12 yards after Dias had fouled the Egyptian.

It was then that Allison's aberrations and Foden's fantasy football took over.

Amazingly Allison sent two clearances straight to City players and from the second of those bloopers, Foden and Gundogan combined again to put us ahead on 73 minutes, with the former feeding the latter.

Just three minutes later it was virtually game-set-and-match when Allison sent a clearance straight to Bernardo, whose cute cross was headed in by Sterling, standing virtually on the goal line.

And Foden capped a brilliant individual performance with the best goal of the game, giving Allison absolutely no chance whatsoever with a magnificent finish on 83 minutes.

KLOPP QUOTES 1 "Alisson made two massive mistakes, gave two goals away – and then a genius situation from Phil Foden."

KLOPP QUOTES 2 "The confidence could have suffered after the last game [a 1-0 home loss against Brighton] but tonight I saw a very confident team, if I'm honest. I liked the football we played. It's very difficult to explain that we lost 4-1."

AND ROY KEANE WEIGHED IN WITH: "Man City showed courage today, bravery to pass forward. Liverpool were the opposite – you talk about champions. They didn't put up a fight in the second half. Man City were outstanding, they were by far the better team. If Liverpool could've won today, it would have been a decent week for them but what a weekend it's been for City. Foden, what a talent."

TOO RISKY Klopp decided not to risk his deadline-day centre-back signings Ben Davies and Ozan Kabak.

PEP QUOTES "For many years we were not able to win here. Hopefully next time we can do it with people [fans in the stadium]."

PENALTY PROBLEMS Four of the past six penalties to have missed the target completely in the Premier League have been by City players, with three of those coming against Liverpool (Mahrez in

CHAPTER 42: ABOUT TIME TOO

October 2018, De Bruyne in November 2020 and Gundogan in this game). In comparison, Liverpool have converted their last 19 Premier pens, with Salah scoring 13 of them.

STERLING WORK Sterling is only the third player to score 100 or more goals under Guardiola, after Barcelona's Lionel Messi (211) and City teammate Aguero (120).

MIND THE GAP Sky Sports' player ratings gave Foden (their man of the match) and Gundogan 9/10 each, with Allison getting 2/10. Presumably, Gundogan would have a 10/10 assessment if he'd scored his penalty!

Chapter 43

WHO'S AFRAID OF THE BIG BAD WOLF?

City 2 Borussia Dortmund 1
Etihad Stadium
Champions League Quarter-final first leg
Tuesday 6 April 2021
Attendance: Nil

City: Ederson, Walker, Dias, Stones, Cancelo, Rodri, Gundogan, Bernardo (Jesus), Foden, Mahrez, De Bruyne. [**De Bruyne, Foden**]

Manager: Pep Guardiola

Borussia Dortmund: Hitz, Morey (Meunier), Hummels, Akanji, Guerreiro, Can, Dahoud (Delaney), Bellingham, Reus, Knauff (Reyna), Haaland. [**Reus**]

BE AFRAID. Be very afraid. Big bad Erling Haaland is in town.

The son of our very own Alf-Inge Haaland, the victim of one of the most notorious tackles in the modern football era, perpetrated by the now rehabilitated (but not in my eyes) Sky pundit Roy Keane.

I watched it again on a grainy YouTube video just to check it was as bad as I thought it was at the time. It was worse.

Keane almost cut Erling's dad in half. It was reminiscent of an IRA knee-capping. Yes, it really was that bad.

Keane got a straight red. Alf-Inge earned a place in football's folklore.

However, contrary to perceived wisdom, it didn't end Alf-Inge's career. Not right away at any rate. In fact, he carried on for the final few minutes of that Manchester derby in 2001; a game that ended all square at 1-1.

Then he played half of a Norway international friendly four days later before featuring for 68 minutes in City's next League game.

But he never featured for the Blues again and underwent surgery to his left knee that summer, although Keane had targeted the right knee.

Alf-Inge never played a full 90 minutes again. Eight years later, he surprisingly resumed his career with Rosseland BK in the Norwegian Third Division, appearing nine times before finally calling it a day.

But let's get back to son of Alf-Inge – and whether he could continue his remarkable record of scoring in every Champions League game of the season.

Of course, you already know the answer to that question if you've been paying attention.

And the reason he didn't was because of the almost impenetrable Stones and Dias combo.

Only once did Haaland the Younger muscle his way past Dias, but the latter stayed with him long enough to just put him off balance a little as he shot and Ederson was able to save in fairly straightforward style.

He did get in good positions and is as strong as an ox, but he was shadowed and shackled brilliantly by the Blues defence.

It's impossible to judge him on one live game – and the second leg, where he also failed to hit the target – but his agent Mino Raiola, the same guy who "looks after" Paul Pogba, went on a tour of possible European destinations with Haaland Senior in the days before this first leg fixture, talking up his 20-year-old client.

Leaving Haaland to one side for the moment, this was another gritty, pragmatic performance from a City side who had to call upon all their inner strengths to grab a vital victory in the dying minutes.

A pinpoint crossfield pass from De Bruyne picked out Gundogan inside the six-yard box and the former Dortmund player offloaded the ball to Foden who swept it home.

City had opened the scoring after a sweeping move, started and finished by De Bruyne, who had seized on a mis-hit pass by Emre Can, and involving Foden and Mahrez.

The ex-Liverpool defender was at the centre of things soon after that opener when Rodri went down clutching his face after a challenge from Can. Referee Ovidiu Hategan pointed to the spot. Rodri may have been kicked, but certainly not in the head, and his theatrical response looked far from credible. After consultation with the VAR, the award was rescinded.

There was even more controversy when former Birmingham City youngster Jude Bellingham appeared to have made it 1-1, but he was adjudged (harshly in my opinion) to have raised his studs to Ederson as he won the ball.

Before Bellingham's shot had crossed the line, the ref blew for a foul, which meant, under the current rules, that VAR couldn't re-visit the incident. I think we got away with one there.

But six minutes from time, Marco Reus did score a legitimate equaliser for the Germans – a precious away goal too.

However, the visitors had reckoned without Foden, ably assisted by Gundogan and De Bruyne. The Blues had been the better team on the night, but had to ride their luck.

And luck had been the missing element in the latter stages of several of Pep's European campaigns with City.

Maybe Lady Luck was finally smiling on us...

DID YOU KNOW? Gundogan was in the Borussia Dortmund team that contested the 2013 Champions League Final against Bayern Munich at Wembley, scoring the equalising goal from the penalty spot in the 69th minute before Dortmund succumbed to a 2-1 defeat.

STERLING OUT Raheem Sterling was a surprise omission from the City starting line-up.

SANCHO OUT Former City Academy starlet Jadon Sancho was missing from the Dortmund line-up through injury. Sancho signed for Man United for £73 million in the 2021 summer transfer window, with City receiving a £10 million windfall as part of the deal. Borussia Dortmund had signed him from City for £8 million. Let's hope he doesn't make us regret letting him go in the first place.

DEAD MAN WALKING Dortmund interim coach Edin Terzic, in the dugout for this game, was appointed after Lucien Favre was sacked in December. But he will make way for Marco Rose, the Borussia Monchengladbach coach, at the end of the season.

PEP'S VIEW: "In the first half we were not clever with the ball but the second half was much better and at 1-0 we had two or three clear chances. Unfortunately, it didn't happen but after we conceded, we got the goal."

YOUNG GUN Foden (20y 313d) became the third-youngest Englishman to score in a Champions League quarter-final, behind Alan Smith in 2001 for Leeds United (20y 158d) and Theo Walcott in 2009 for Arsenal (20y 30d).

DE BEST? De Bruyne has been directly involved in 13 goals in his last 12 Champions League matches (four goals, nine assists) and has scored four goals and assisted three more in seven starts in Champions League quarter-final games.

Chapter 44

BREAKING DOWN THE WALL

Borussia Dortmund 1 City 2
Signal Iduna Park
Champions League Quarter-final Second leg
Wednesday 14 April 2021
Attendance: Nil

Borussia Dortmund: Hitz, Morey (Tigges), Akanji, Hummels, Guerreiro, Bellingham (Brandt), Can, Dahoud (T Hazard), Knauff (Reyna), Haaland, Reus. [**Bellingham**]

City: Ederson, Walker, Stones, Dias, Zinchenko, De Bruyne, Rodri, Gündogan, Mahrez (Sterling), Bernardo, Foden. [**Mahrez** pen, **Foden**]

Manager: Pep Guardiola

PHIL SPECTOR may have been a convicted murderer who was still in prison when he died earlier in the year, but he *was* a musical genius and his lasting legacy was the Wall of Sound.

Borussia Dortmund have their own wall of sound – the Yellow Wall – but with Covid-19 ruling out crowds, it was a massive bonus for the Blues that Signal Iduna Park was empty apart from players, media and assorted officials.

Dortmund's 81,365-capacity stadium can be a scary place for visiting sides and they also boast the highest average attendance in world football.

In the pre-pandemic season of 2019-20, Dortmund sold out an astonishing 99.7 per cent of their seats for Bundesliga games – that's an average crowd of 81,154.

Even without their fanatical backing they were first to strike in this tense quarter-final with Jude Bellingham – at 17 almost a child prodigy compared with our own Phil Foden – beating Ederson, who got a hand to the powerful, well-placed shot, but not a strong enough hand.

Stones, who had stuttered in recent weeks, including for England, after a stellar season, got wrong side of Erling Haaland and the Norwegian's cross found its way to Bellingham, who brilliantly made space for himself before firing home.

So, 15 minutes in and we were back on level terms and as it stood the Germans were going through to the semi-finals courtesy of their away goal the previous week.

De Bruyne went close to putting us back in front in the tie, striking the bar in the first half with Hitz nowhere near, and then Bellingham popped up in his own penalty area to kick the ball off the line from a Mahrez shot after Foden had shown amazing skill and awareness to keep the ball in play.

Bellingham, the Stourbridge-born ex-Birmingham City youngster, celebrated as though he had scored another goal, such was Dortmund's determination to keep their noses in front.

But the Blues breakthrough came on 54 minutes when Emre Can was adjudged to have handled a Foden cross. The referee pointed straight to the spot, but there was a lengthy wait while VAR checked the decision. Eventually they confirmed the arbiter had made the right call.

From some angles it looked as though Can may have headed the ball onto his arm, but the arm was in a stretched-out, unnatural position and Mahrez stepped up to take the kick.

The City winger remained as cool as the weather and blasted a brilliant penalty past Hitz's despairing dive. We were level on the night and in front in the tie.

De Bruyne again went close, but City weren't to be denied and Foden, from just outside the box, beat the Dortmund keeper with the ball ricocheting off the post and into the net.

Some critics thought Hitz might have done better, but the ball was arrowed into the corner and all credit to Foden for taking the shot on.

As soon as the ball crossed the line, Foden was off and running – to embrace an ecstatic Guardiola on the touchline.

It was a show of how much Pep means to Phil and vice versa with the former Barcelona and Bayern boss having gone on record that the 'Stockport Iniesta' was the greatest talent he had ever worked with. Some recommendation from one of the greatest managers in the game's history.

Pep had been criticised by some fans and pundits who had claimed that his policy of bringing Foden along slowly was stifling the player's progress. Many of these so-called experts had been vocal in suggesting that he should have gone out on loan.

But Pep stood firm and was proved right. Foden is a generational talent, make no mistake about that, and who knows just how good he will be in say three-five, ten years' time. If he was to improve only five per cent a year, he could rival the all-time greats like Christiano Ronaldo and Lionel Messi. It's certainly going to be an interesting journey.

DID YOU KNOW? Staggeringly, Bayern Munich beat even Borussia Dortmund's percentage ticket sales in 2019-20, selling out every single game at their Allianz Arena, according to official Bundesliga figures, giving them an average crowd of 75,000 in their 75,000-capacity state-of-the-art stadium.

RIYAD ON THE SPOT Mahrez famously missed a late penalty in City's 0-0 draw in the 2018-19 season against Liverpool, blasting the ball way over the bar. Prior to that, he had failed in five of his eight attempts from the spot in top-flight games. But the Algerian now seems to be getting the hang of taking penalties, at least in the Champions League... his spot kick in this game was his third success in a row in the competition.

IT'S GOOD TO TALK Just as they had done after the first leg in Manchester, the cameras picked out Foden and Haaland chatting to each other after the final whistle. City fans would love to have heard what they actually said. Probably, 'well played' from Phil, rather than, 'see you in sky blue next season'! But who knows?

RECORD EQUALLED Pep has reached his eighth Champions League semi-final, now the joint-most in the history of the competition among all managers, alongside Jose Mourinho.

WHAT THE GAFFER SAID: "I'm incredibly happy for this club, the chairman, the players, the fans. We were brilliant except for the first 10 minutes."

Chapter 45

ONE-WAY TRAFFIC

City 1 Tottenham Hotspur 0
Wembley Stadium
Carabao Cup Final
Sunday 25 April 2021
Attendance: 7,773

City: Steffen, Walker, Dias, Laporte, Cancelo, Fernandinho (Rodri 84), Gundogan, Mahrez, De Bruyne (Bernardo 87), Sterling, Foden. [**Laporte**]

Manager: Pep Guardiola

Spurs: Lloris, Aurier (Bergwijn), Alderweireld, Dier, Reguilon, Winks, Hojbjerg (Alli), Lo Celso (Sissoko), Moura (Bale), Kane, Son.

ABOUT 2,000 City fans made it to Wembley for the annual Carabao Cup Final presentation ceremony. Sadly, I wasn't one of them so I didn't get to see the Blues win the trophy for a record-breaking fourth successive season.

As a CEV – Clinically Extremely Vulnerable – person, according to the NHS, I wasn't even allowed to apply for a ticket, so I'm going to cheat a little and reintroduce my healthier/younger brother, Adrian, whom you may remember from the first chapter back in 1956.

He actually got his hands on a ticket, took a Covid test 24 hours before kick-off as part of the government's Event Research Programme, and strolled down a far-from-crowded Wembley Way.

Incidentally, back in the day, I always felt one needed to be tested to be a City fan, so nothing new there then.

Adrian reckoned it was like attending a Premier League away game, where our allocation would have been marginally bigger, certainly at the larger stadiums on the circuit.

All told, there were 7,773 spectators in attendance – the limit had been set at 8,000 in this Covid test event – with 2,000 tickets for each of the finalists and the rest to NHS personnel and Brent residents. However, the official crowd figure didn't include the additional 11 spectators in the Spurs starting line-up, plus their four substitutes and the rest of their bench.

For, truth be told, the north London team didn't turn up, well not on the pitch, especially the much-vaunted Kane-Son alliance, which barely got a sniff all game thanks to the dominance of our well-drilled defence, ably led by the rock-like Ruben Dias.

Right from the off City were as positive – the polar opposite to their supporters' negative Covid tests – and it ended up as one of the most one-sided 1-0 wins of the season.

It might have been any score you like if City had not been so profligate in front of goal, missing chance after chance – as well as missing a recognised striker. Injury-plagued substitute Aguero, running down the clock on his iconic ten-year City story, had trained only once in the week prior to the game, while Jesus doesn't appear to fit in on a regular basis as Pep continues to use a collection of false nines.

Brother Adrian confirmed what we all saw on TV that there wasn't a lot of social distancing in the crowd, a bit like the packed Spurs defence as they tried ever so hard to keep us out.

And, in fact, it took 82 minutes until the dam was breached and it was a defender, Aymeric Laporte, who did the breaching, netting with a header from a De Bruyne free-kick after Sterling had been bowled over in a reckless challenge by Serge Aurier.

That was the signal for commentator Martin Tyler and his sidekick Gary Neville to immediately refer to the fact that Laporte shouldn't have been on the pitch at all, never mind scoring the only goal of the game.

Yes, he should have been booked for a tactical-type foul on Lucas Moura in the 25th minute, but he wasn't. He was then yellow carded for a similar foul on the same player in the 45th minute. But surely, it's not too much of a stretch to believe that Laporte wouldn't have committed his second foul if he had been shown a yellow for the first.

What was lucky about Laporte's starring role was that he probably wouldn't have played if John Stones hadn't been sent off at Aston Villa a few days earlier.

There was no sentimental five-minute cameo for Aguero as Guardiola swapped Fernandinho for Rodri for the last knockings. But, true to his attacking ethos, there no sense we were shutting up shop and the Blues kept on attacking until the final whistle.

City should have been home and dry well before then with Mahrez, in particular, unlucky not to score, in addition to Foden, De Bruyne, Sterling and Gundogan.

For Spurs, goalkeeper Lloris and defenders Hojbjerg and Alderweireld came out of the game with credit – among the few in white shirts to do so.

STATS WHY WE WON City's expected goals (xG) total was a pretty high 3.63, from 21 shots, while Spurs xG was a staggeringly low 0.06 from two shots.

NO JOSE Spurs sacked manager Jose Mourinho, a four-time winner of the League Cup, six days before the game – on the same day that the ill-fated European Super League was announced. That left 29-year-old former Spurs player Ryan Mason in charge of the side. It was his second game in the hot seat after the midweek win over Southampton.

FINAL COUNTDOWN For Pep it was a remarkable 14th win in 15 major finals – four League Cups and an FA Cup with City; three out of three with Barcelona and six from seven at Bayern Munich.

BIGGEST CHEER OF THE DAY Fans in the Spurs end erupted in the 18th minute when the side won its first corner. It sounded more ironic than anything else, a bit like the sort of noise you would hear from League Two fans during a cup-tie at a Premier League ground.

PRIVILEGED PRESS There were printed programmes for the media, but none available at the ground for the fans due to Covid fears. They can, however, be purchased on various websites including eBay.

DID YOU KNOW? City met Spurs at the new Wembley in a Premier League encounter in April 2018 when Tottenham were using the national stadium as their temporary "home" after disputes and delays had beset the building of the replacement for White Hart Lane. Spurs' new ground was finally opened a year after that game, which City won 3-1 to move within three points of the League title. We also met them at Wembley in October the same year, winning 1-0. At the time of writing, Spurs new ground is still called the Tottenham Hotspur Stadium, with the club yet to sell the naming rights.

Chapter 46

A WALK IN THE PARC

Paris Saint-Germain 1 City 2
Parc des Princes
Champions League Semi-final First leg
Wednesday 28 April 2021
Attendance: Nil

City: Ederson, Walker, Stones, Dias, Cancelo, (Zinchenko), Bernardo, Rodri, Gündogan, Mahrez, De Bruyne, Foden. [**De Bruyne, Mahrez**]

Manager: Pep Guardiola

Paris Saint-Germain: Navas, Florenzi, Marquinhos, Kimpembe, Bakke, Gueye, Paredes (Herrera), Di María (Danilo), Neymar, Verratti, Mbappé. [**Marquinhos**]

LET'S first of all deal with the 'Elephant in the Room' or rather the 'Oil Tanker on the Touchline'.

To all intents and purposes, both of these clubs are well oiled as well as state-owned and in the build-up the air was thick, particularly in some branches of the print and social media, with mentions of 'petrodollars' and 'sportswashing' agendas.

Abu Dhabi, ultimate owners and benefactors of City since 2008, have a far from spotless record on human rights abuses, while the Qatar regime that bought PSG three years later has had the dark, swirling clouds of bribery and corruption hanging over it ever since the country was awarded the 2022 World Cup.

Now that we've sort of dealt with where the teams are coming from, we'll focus on the match itself.

The phrase 'a game of two halves' has become a footballing cliché that has gone well beyond the confines of the sport itself, but it really did sum up this semi-final clash.

After a promising enough first 10 minutes or so when we had plenty of possession, PSG then threatened to overwhelm us.

And it was no surprise when they went ahead as early as the 14th minute after Marquinhos ran across the City defence at a corner and expertly nodded the ball past Ederson.

Clearly, the worst possible start.

We tried to get a foothold in the game and Bernardo, fed a great ball by Cancelo, went close not long afterwards, but Navas was alert to the threat at his near post.

However, with Neymar and Mbappe turning us inside out at times, it was the French side who were bossing the show.

Even so, we could have been level just before the interval when Foden found himself in space. Either side of the keeper and he would have scored, but he drilled his shot straight at the former Real Madrid stopper.

Twenty minutes later, Navas was thanking his lucky stars that De Bruyne's fabulous overhead kick flew just over the bar on 60 minutes as City came out all guns blazing in the second half. It would have been one of the goals of the tournament had it been a few inches below the bar instead of a few inches over it.

De Bruyne did beat Navas three minutes later, though, when the 34-year-old Costa Rican was left in no man's land after KDB had floated one towards the far post.

No one got on the end of it and the keeper was left cursing as it curled into the corner.

PSG, basically flat track bullies in Ligue 1 with six title wins in the last eight seasons at the time of writing, were beginning to unravel.

Implode is probably a better word to describe them and City were happy to take full advantage. Foden won a free-kick in a fairly central position just outside the box and De Bruyne and Mahrez were in conversation over the ball for quite a while before the Algerian decided he'd give it a try.

In fairness, the free-kick was poor, straight into the wall, but two PSG players, Mbappe and Paredes, parted like the Red Sea, and Mahrez's effort whistled past Navas to make it 2-1 for the Blues.

It was a bit of good fortune, but as the late, great film producer Samuel Goldwyn famously said, 'the harder I work the luckier I get', and how many times in the past has Lady Luck scowled rather than smiled on City's efforts, more often than not in this competition.

Further evidence of PSG's disintegration came soon afterwards when the former Everton defender Idrissa Gueye was shown a straight red for a heinous challenge on Gundogan, who appeared lucky to escape serious injury. There was no escape for Gueye, though, he was off down the tunnel without protest.

City had defended resolutely in a first half where they had been under the cosh for long periods. But they were able to play a much more free-flowing game in the second half as PSG wilted under the pressure.

FAIR COMMENT Gary Lineker tweeted to his 7.9 million followers: "That was one of the best performances, in an away leg, by an English side in the history of European football. Absolutely outstanding."

DICKOV'S VIEW "A world-class performance from a world-class team."

WHAT THE BOSSES THOUGHT Guardiola said: "We didn't have good possession in the right positions. This club don't have much experience in the semi-finals of this tournament. This will help us. In the second half we were aggressive and played really good.

"Against Dortmund [in the quarter-final], we conceded and came back. Today the same. [We were] ourselves in the second half. We are good playing in a certain way. We can't do a different way."

PSG gaffer **Mauricio Pochettino**, who had guided Spurs to the 2018-19 CL final, said: "There were two different halves – we did well in the first half but it is difficult to eliminate a team like City. We deserved to be ahead but they were better than us and dominated the second half. The two goals were accidents, but they created more than us. It was one half for each team.

"The two goals are very disappointing. It is difficult to accept but that can happen, and it has happened in a semi-final. It is very painful.

"It is difficult to explain why they were better but we were better in the first half. It was difficult to cope, their physical condition, they were more aggressive. We didn't show the energy you need. The red card could be yellow, could be red."

AWAY DAY JOY City's victory meant they had won their past 18 away matches in all competitions, scoring 46 goals and conceding just nine.

KING KEVIN De Bruyne has been directly involved in nine goals in his past eight Champions League appearances in the knockout stage (five goals, four assists). He became the fourth City player to reach double figures for Champions League goals after Sergio Aguero (36), Raheem Sterling (21) and Gabriel Jesus (16).

KEEPING GOOD COMPANY KDB became the fourth different player to score in three consecutive Champions League matches against PSG, after Lionel Messi, Marcus Rashford and Neymar (four).

DID YOU KNOW? For the first three years of its existence, PSG was fan-owned with 20,000 members.

Chapter 47

SNOW DANGER

City 2 Paris Saint-Germain 0
(City won 4-1 on aggregate)
Etihad Stadium
Champions League Semi-final Second leg
Tuesday 4 May 2021
Attendance: Nil

City: Ederson, Walker, Stones, Dias, Zinchenko, Mahrez, Fernandinho, Gündogan, Foden (Agüero). De Bruyne, (Jesus), Bernardo (Sterling). [**Mahrez** 2]

Manager: Pep Guardiola

Paris Saint-Germain: Navas, Florenzi (Dagbaat), Marquinhos, Kimpembe, Diallo (Bakker) Herrera (Draxler), Paredes, (Danilo), Verratti, Di María, Icardi (Kean), Neymar.

BIZARRELY there was a slight danger that this early May fixture, one of the biggest in the club's history, might have been called off because of snow and hail.

About an hour before kick-off, there were videos on Twitter showing the referee checking 'the roll of the ball' on the surface of the pitch.

But a possible postponement was avoided and the match went ahead as planned with all lines visible after work by the ground staff.

Bizarrely again, it wasn't until the half-time interval that an attempt was made to clear away all the snow – and even then, the "sweepers" were forced to call it a day after running out of time, leaving one part of the pitch, to the left of Ederson's goal, still covered in the white stuff.

From kick-off, it took a while for the teams to get used to the slightly slippery playing surface, but PSG appeared to settle the better of the two sides.

Starting without the injured Mbappe, PSG's bright start saw them awarded a penalty after just six minutes.

Thankfully, VAR got it right overruling the ref's decision – a fairly straightforward decision with the ball striking Zinchenko's shoulder.

Four minutes later and Zinchenko was involved again as a wonderfully accurate long ball from Ederson found the Ukrainian who had waited inside his own half to avoid an offside flag before taking the ball in his stride. Three times he looked for De Bruyne who had raced forward at the same time, eventually finding him with a pinpoint pass. De Bruyne's shot was charged down, but the ball broke to Mahrez and he did the rest, keeping the effort low to get it past Navas.

But even though they were now 3-1 down in the tie, PSG always looked dangerous and former United attacker Angel Di Maria won the ball back after a quick throw from Ederson had put Gundogan in trouble. But the Argentine, who had an unhappy time at Old Trafford, looked no happier here after hitting the ball wide of an open goal.

PSG still swarmed forward with City's defenders, Zinchenko, Walker, Stones and the superlative Dias blocking shot after shot. They simply put their bodies on the line and as a result of their bravery, Ederson barely had a shot to deal with.

Borussia Dortmund may have a Yellow Wall; we now have a Blue Wall and how effective it was.

And it was one of the bricks in that Blue Wall that started the move that brought us the goal that settled the tie on 62 minutes.

Zinchenko found De Bruyne, who interchanged passes with Foden, and the latter's cross picked out the unmarked Mahrez, who slammed the ball into the roof of the net. 2-0 on the night. 4-1 on aggregate. Game over.

But the drama was far from over.

Six minutes after PSG suffered that crushing blow, Di Maria was shown a straight red after a petulant stamp on a prostrate Fernandinho.

The Brazilian, who celebrated his 36th birthday on match day, had a "handbags at ten paces" exchange with the former United man, who then stamped on Ferna's ankle just before taking a PSG throw-in.

Away from the mayhem, Foden almost capped a brilliant night with a goal when, after a balletic turn enabled him to lose his marker, he shot against the post with Navas beaten.

Back to the madness and PSG's Kimpembe was extremely fortunate to stay on the field after a truly shocking "tackle" on Jesus in the closing stages as the French side completely lost their cool. Presumably, Kimpembe's yellow was checked by VAR, but no further sanction was ordered.

PSG could easily have ended the game with eight men, while City were glad to get off the field without any serious injuries as they booked a place in the Champions League final for the first time in their history.

LATE ON PARADE Did PSG deliberately delay the start of the second half? City were out and ready to go about three minutes before all of the French side finally made it onto the field according to my guesstimate, with Neymar the last to join the party. He was seen on BT Sport's tunnel camera, tying his bootlaces and putting on his gloves about two minutes after the scheduled restart. On that coverage, the referee can be seen giving a quizzical look to one of his assistants as PSG appeared to tarry. Maybe Pochettino was giving a lengthy team talk and forgot to look at his watch or maybe he was trying to gain some sort of psychological advantage as City shivered on the pitch eager for the match to resume.

PSG have some previous here. Former coach Thomas Tuchel, now of course in charge of Chelsea, was warned "for being responsible for the late kick-off" for the second half of their Champions League quarter-final against Atalanta. The club was fined £27,000. That time the late show did the trick as PSG overturned a 1-0 half-time deficit to triumph 2-1.

As far as I know, no investigation was carried out into this possible breach, but one should remember that in 2012 City were fined around £24,000 (30,000 euros) by UEFA for being "up to one minute" late onto the pitch at Porto in a CL tie; the same tie that brought a £16,000 (20,000 euros) fine for Porto after their fans' racist chants at Yaya Toure and Mario Balotelli.

RED MIST Di Maria's red card was the tenth of the season in all competitions for PSG. The French champions had three players sent off, including Neymar and Paredes, in their 1-0 home Ligue 1 defeat by Marseille in September 2020, with the visitors receiving two reds. Incredibly, all five players were dismissed in stoppage time.

DIRTY DOZEN Clearly Kimpembe hadn't cooled down by the following Sunday when he was sent off in a 1-1 draw with Rennes – PSG's eleventh red card of the season.

WHAT PEP SAID: "They put a lot of players in the middle and we struggled a lot in the first half to high press and we changed at half time. We recovered the ball better in the second half and we were much better in the way we played and 4-1 on aggregate against a team that beat Barcelona and Bayern Munich means a lot to us."

SEVEN-UP City's success was their seventh consecutive Champions League victory, the longest winning run by an English team in European Cup/Champions League history. Two other sides had won six in a row: Manchester United (1965-66) and Leeds United (1969-70).

Chapter 48

IT'S TIME TO SAY GOODBYE

City 5 Everton 0
Etihad Stadium
Premier League
Sunday 23 May 2021
Attendance: 10,000

City: Ederson, Walker, Stones, Dias, Zinchenko, De Bruyne, Fernandinho, Foden (Rodri), Mahrez (Aguero), Jesus (Torres), Sterling. [**De Bruyne, Jesus, Foden, Aguero** 2]

Manager: Pep Guardiola

Everton: Pickford, Digne, Godfrey, Keane, Holgate, Davies, Allan, Doucoure (Iwobi), Sigurdsson (Bernard), Richarlison (Nkounkou), Calvert-Lewin

---

SERGIO KUN AGUERO introduced himself to the City faithful on 15 August 2011, a mere 3,569 days before this fixture.

In those three-and-a-half thousand-plus days, apart from a couple of petulant tackles, he hasn't offered up even the semblance of a problem to his employers or his adoring fans.

Few players at elite level can say that in a stellar career lasting more than a decade.

So, we must salute the Argentinian for his durability as well as his score-ability.

His two-goal cameo in this game brought his Premier League total to 184, eclipsing Wayne Rooney's record of 183 for a single club.

Aguero is the club's record goalscorer too, with 260, miles ahead of Eric Brook (1927-1940) on 177 and Tommy Johnson (1920-1930) who scored 166 times. The great Colin Bell (1966-1979) is in fourth on the all-time list with 153 alongside Joe Hayes (1953-1965).

I have set out some of Aguero's other records below.

It's often said of a departing club legend, 'We'll never see his like again'. In Sergio's case, I am afraid that is true. Even Harry Kane or Erling Haaland, or both of them, wouldn't do the trick for me.

And as if to prove the point, Aguero did what he does best in this game, neatly bookending his Premier League career with a two-goal appearance from off the bench just as he did on debut against Swansea.

Here, he replaced Mahrez after 65 minutes, and netted our fourth (71 minutes) and fifth (76 minutes).

Against Swansea, manager Roberto Mancini sent on the fresh-faced Argentine and he made an instant hit scoring one predatory goal and another spectacular one as the Blues battered the Swans 4-0. It was a taste of things to come.

Of course, he will always be remembered for that Aguerooo moment when his goal clinched the League title for us on 93 minutes 20 seconds in 2012 (see Chapter 26), but the man shouldn't be defined for that moment even though it was one of the most life-changing goals in the club's history.

He did much, much more than that. His goals – especially those against top opposition in crucial matches – just kept on coming.

In this current season, he had been dogged by Covid and injury and was rarely fully fit. Pep decided to let him go and he has gone to Barcelona, where I hope he flourishes although at the time of writing another injury is keeping him out of the Barca line-up. Few will deny him one last hurrah.

Pep was in tears at the final whistle as the pair embraced, but their relationship back in the dressing room and on the training ground might not always have been so harmonious.

But all differences – supposed and real – were forgotten as he stepped up to receive his fifth Premier League winner's medal as the team celebrated with the fans at the finish.

The game itself was a bit of a stroll against an Everton team that looked as though they weren't all that bothered after a season where they had flattered to deceive – and not for the first time.

De Bruyne, despite momentarily losing his footing, picked his spot from range to make it 1-0. Jesus added a second with a well-taken effort and Foden showed sublime skills to grab a third – before super sub Aguero closed the show with two goals in a five-minute spell, only six minutes after joining the fray; aided it must be said, by some poor Everton marking.

A special mention for Ederson, who saved a Sigurdsson penalty (given away by Dias who brought down Richarlison) and for Walker who blocked the follow-up from Richarlison who was the first Everton player to get to the ball.

GET HIM ON Fernandinho, spotting that Aguero was on the touchline and ready to come on, told Mahrez to put the ball out of play. And it was Fernandinho who provided the assists for both Aguero goals.

A RECORD NUMBER OF RECORDS Aguero set so many records during his City career that there isn't enough space to mention them all. Here are some of them: Most goals scored in all competitions (260); most matches scored in (186); most braces in our history (37); most hat-tricks (16) and probably the most significant record, most goals against the Big Six (52 in 91 games).

He was also the only non-UK player in the top nine City goalscorers of all time. Seven of them were English with one Welshman (Billy Meredith) and one Scot (Billie Gillespie) in the list.

Joe Hayes, whose path I used to cross most mornings as I went to school and as he got the bus to training at Maine Road – he'd obviously left his Lamborghini in the drive back home – was the fifth highest City scorer at the time of writing with 153 goals, equal with Colin Bell. Joe was kind enough to get me tickets to some games. Can you imagine that happening in the current era?

CARLO CRUSHED Everton manager Carlo Ancelotti suffered the heaviest defeat in his 1,167-game managerial career – and just ten days later he was gone, having left the Toffees to take over from the departing Zinedine Zidane at Real Madrid. The Italian had previously managed the Spanish club from 2013-2015, winning the Champions League in 2014.

PAYING THE PENALTY The Blues had conceded 10 penalties in the 1920-21 season – the most in a Premier League campaign.

SWEET JESUS Gabriel Jesus made it eight goals in eight PL games against Everton, more than he has scored against any other opponent.

Chapter 49

WE PLAYED LIKE PENSIONERS!

City 0 Chelsea 1
Estadio do Dragao, Porto
Champions League Final
Saturday 29 May 2021
Attendance: 14,110

City: Ederson, Walker, Stones, Dias, Zinchenko, Bernardo (Fernandinho), Gundogan, Foden, Mahrez, De Bruyne (Jesus), Sterling (Aguero).

Manager: Pep Guardiola

Chelsea: Mendy, Azpilicueta, Thiago Silver (Christensen), Rudiger, James, Kante, Jorginho, Chilwell, Havertz, Mount (Kovacic), Werner (Pulisic). [**Havertz**]

THREE (fairly invasive and expensive) Covid tests, two plane journeys, one (very pricey) match ticket and no goals. Oh, and no holding midfielder. That's basically the story of City's first appearance in the Champions League Final.

I would actually like to stop right now and write no more, but that would be a dereliction of duty on my part and short-change you, the reader.

So, let's start at the very beginning, as they sing in Do Re Mi in the *Sound of Music*.

Firstly, a huge vote of thanks to City owner Sheikh Mansour who footed the bill for 15 return flights from Manchester for about 3,000 Blues fans.

I wasn't able to take advantage of the sheikh's generous offer as I was travelling from London, but getting there wasn't as much of a hassle as I thought it might be once the two pre-trip Covid tests had been done and all the paperwork and online shenanigans had been completed.

Queues outward bound were manageable, but Porto airport was a bit of shambles with only three non-EU desks to deal with the hundreds of fans (all from the UK) as well as hundreds of other ordinary travellers who just happened to be on their way to a holiday in Portugal.

But it was on arrival in Porto itself that things got even more shambolic with taxi queues stretching for what seemed like miles.

I turned down the first guy to approach me with an offer of a taxi because I thought he might be dodgy/unlicensed, but when he reappeared by which time the queue hadn't moved an inch, I thought what have I got to lose.

He turned out to be a real gent and told me the only reason he couldn't join the rank was because he wasn't from Porto, but he had a spotlessly clean Mercedes and transported a lot of footballers to Lisbon, including Nicolas Otamendi, bringing a new meaning to the phrase 'Taxi for Otamendi'. He even mentioned that he knew Bruno Fernandes who used to live in the adjoining village. I told him that personally I'd never heard of Fernandes, but I don't think he believed me.

Once I'd reached my hotel and checked in, I took a stroll around the city centre and was pleasantly surprised at just how happy and trouble-free the two sets of fans were as they mingled in the May sunshine although there had been reports of skirmishes between fans and police when they closed down a number of watering holes due to Covid regulations the previous day.

But my taxi ride and the carefree atmosphere in town and later around the ground was about as good as it got.

The first bit of bad news came when the teams were announced. I couldn't see either Fernandinho or Rodri in any midfield role and, to my amazement, Sterling was back in the starting line-up after one of his worst runs of form in a blue shirt. For a little while, I actually thought there were only ten names on the team sheet.

I checked again and even asked a couple of people sitting nearby, just to confirm I wasn't seeing things or even going off my rocker, but I was told that *was* the team in its entirety.

The aforementioned Sterling could have given us a dream start in the ninth minute when he brilliantly anticipated a superb long pass from Ederson, but his first touch let him down and despite recovering he just doesn't score in one-on-one situations and we had to settle for a corner that came to naught.

In truth, City never got going and nor did their fans in the 14,000 crowd. City crowds at home have a reputation for being more reactive than proactive, responding to great performances or passages of play although some particularly important matches down the years have disproved this theory.

City's away support is usually a different kettle of fish altogether, but I sensed that, just like the team, they simply never got into their stride.

Without a midfield anchor, Pep had set us up for all-out attack, but it never happened; De Bruyne and Gundogan seemingly unsure of their exact roles in this new formation and almost from the off there was an air of resignation among the Blues supporters.

It's not that we played badly, it was that we were well below our exceptionally high standards.

At kick-off we were Champions League Final "virgins" and if excuses are sought – apart from the usual 'Pep's over-thought it again' line – then it should be noted that of the last 11 teams to play in their first final, only one, Borussia Dortmund, have achieved success, beating Juventus 3-1 in 1997.

On this night though, a single goal scored minutes before the interval by Kai Havertz, his first in the competition, separated the two sides.

For the most part, the Pensioners' well-marshalled defence, with Kante in imperious form, snuffed out our attacking intent and when Antonio Rudiger took out De Bruyne in the 54th minute, damaging the Belgian's eye socket and breaking his nose, it looked like game over. Rudiger received a yellow; on another night it might have been a red and then who knows?

Fernandinho replaced De Bruyne and then on came Sergio Aguero, in place of the misfiring Sterling, for his last hurrah in a City shirt, but he seemed to be chasing shadows for what little remained of the second half and there was to be no fairy tale ending to his iconic Etihad career.

That evening in Porto was a quiet one; the journey home even quieter. But we will learn from this and, hopefully, come back stronger.

BOGEY TEAM? Pep has lost more matches against Chelsea in all competitions than against any other club (eight), losing his last three in a row against the west London side. The only other teams he has lost three in a row against in his managerial career are Real Madrid (2012-14) and Liverpool (2018).

NO. 9 City became the ninth different English team to reach a European Cup/Champions League final.

THE FINAL STRAW: Guardiola has lost his first cup final as City manager, with this loss only the second major cup final defeat on his managerial CV (along with the Copa del Rey final in 2010-11). In the latter match, Real Madrid beat Pep's Barcelona team 1-0 with a goal in extra time from Cristiano Ronaldo.

NOT EVEN CLOSE Following Havertz's goal in the 42nd minute neither side managed to land a single shot on target during the rest of the match.

Chapter 50

NO KANE, NO PROBLEM

City 5 Arsenal 0
Etihad Stadium
Premier League – Saturday 28 August 2021
Attendance: 52,276

City: Ederson, Walker (Zinchenko), Dias, Laporte, Cancelo, Bernardo (Sterling), Rodri, Gundogan, Jesus (Mahrez), Torres, Grealish. [**Torres 2, Gundogan, Jesus, Rodri**]

Manager: Pep Guardiola

Arsenal: Leno, Chambers, Holding, Kolasinac, Soares, Xhaka, Smith-Rowe, Tierney, Saka (Elneny), Odegaard (Maitland-Niles), Aubameyang (Lacazette).

NO KANE, no Ronaldo, no De Bruyne, no Foden. No problem.

The game kicked off less than 24 hours after Ronaldo (or, most probably, his agent) had decided that Manchester United were a better proposition than City and in the same week that the Blues summer-long pursuit of Harry Kane had finally been ended by Spurs intransigent chairman Daniel Levy.

It also saw a line-up that was shorn of two of our biggest stars – De Bruyne and Foden – through injury, but it mattered not a jot as Arsenal were taken apart piece by piece.

Had referee Martin Atkinson been appointed by the British Boxing Board of Control and not the Premier League, he would have stopped the contest long before the final whistle.

Come to think of it, this was never a 'contest', it was a stroll in the sunshine as Arsenal folded like an unwanted deckchair.

For the first five or six minutes the Gunners, despite missing several big players themselves, were on the front foot, mainly throwing long balls forward, but from City's first attack in the seventh minute, the ball was in the back of the net with Gundogan, in a fair amount of space, heading home from a Jesus cross.

Five minutes later Torres took advantage of some terrible defending, with the ball getting to him past the flailing efforts of three Arsenal defenders, allowing him to steer it past Leno.

And it got better.

Xhaka made a crude, out-of-control, studs-up challenge on Cancelo and was handed a straight red. With eleven men, Arsenal couldn't contain City. With 10, it was an impossible task.

And so it proved with a third before the break. This time Grealish, looking as though he is enjoying every moment of his nascent City career, worked his magic along the byline before crossing for Jesus to grab his first goal of the season.

Although this was a typical striker's goal, I have long felt the Brazilian had looked better cutting in from the right rather than when in a No.9 role – and so it proved in the opening games of the 2021-22 campaign. Whether Pep keeps him out wide – his role for Brazil – or switches him back to spearhead the attack remains to be seen.

At 3-0, the game was won, but there were two more nails hammered into the Arsenal coffin after the interval; the first a superbly well-taken strike from Rodri and the second, another for Torres via a well-directed header.

The statues of City greats Vincent Kompany and David Silva, which had been unveiled outside the ground earlier in the day, had probably shown more movement than the majority of this humiliated Arsenal team.

Personally, I felt sorry for Arsenal boss Mikel Arteta, now in his second full season at the club after leaving his role as Pep's assistant. He did some great work at the Etihad, but maybe stepping straight into the cauldron that is the Premier League as a head coach isn't such a good idea. From sorcerer's apprentice to sorcerer is a big, big step.

Guardiola also showed sympathy for his former colleague, saying: "They have six or seven players injured and at two-zero they have a player sent off – it is a big advantage for us."

UNCHANGED MELODY Pep, whose team selection tweaks are the stuff of Fantasy Football nightmares, picked the same team for successive top-flight fixtures for the first time since October 2017, almost four years earlier.

TAKE YOUR PICK BBC Sport gave the Player of the Match award to Jack Grealish; City gave the Man of the Match award to Ferran Torres while BT Sport who covered the match handed their accolade to Ilkay Gundogan (via ex-Arsenal stalwart Martin Keown) and Sky Sports, who didn't cover the match, made it two votes for Torres.

STATS THE WAY TO DO IT Unsurprisingly, City won all of the key stats battles – 25 shots against Arsenal's single effort; ten shots on target against the Gunners total of zero and 14-0 on the corner count. Percentage-wise possession was 80-20 in favour of the Blues, yet the most telling metric was City's pass success rate of 91% against the visitors' 67%.

TERRIBLE START Defeat meant that the Gunners had fired blanks in their first three PL games, losing all three and failing to garner a single point – their worst start in 67 years.

TOILET PERFORMANCE Arsenal fans were heading for the exits after about 35 minutes. Yes, the toilets do get crowded if you wait for the half-time whistle, but it's not that bad. Maybe they were on their way home...

5-0 5-0 5-0 City repeated the feat of winning three consecutive Premier League home games 5-0. They had achieved it previously in October 2017, while Chelsea managed it in August 2010.

SEEING RED Xhaka's dismissal was the eleventh red card of his career and since Arteta left the Blues to manage Arsenal in December 2019 the north Londoners' disciplinary record has been the worst in the league with 11 early baths, four more than any other club.

UP-AND-DOWN EDERSON City's Brazilian shot-stopper had a strange game. He was far too casual when he almost gifted a goal to Smith-Rowe, with the rebound off the Arsenal midfielder's boot proving to be the visitors' only attempt on goal of the entire game although, in my book, it hardly qualified as a shot. And several times in the first half he took so much time releasing the ball that his manager vented his frustration from the touchline. Ed even kicked the ball out of play when under no pressure. But he more than made amends for his out-of-character performance when he threaded a magnificent pass through to Torres which culminated in the Jesus goal. Perhaps he was bored he had so little to do...

Bonus Chapter

WITH GRATEFUL THANKS

Manchester United 1 Leicester City 2
Old Trafford
Premier League
Tuesday 11 May 2021

DON'T worry, you haven't suddenly strayed into the wrong book.

This is the moment when City's Premier League crown was returned to its rightful owner.

This is the moment when United's 'We'll delay City's title' bandwagon came to a juddering halt.

Of course, Fred Done, founder of Betfred bookmakers and a lifelong Red, had paid out on City back in March when there were 11 games still to play. The Blues held a 14-point lead at the time, but Mr Done reckoned that the publicity was worth way more than any money he had to pay out if he got it wrong and had to fork out twice.

And yes, United manager Ole Gunner Solskjaer made no fewer than 10 changes from the side that had beaten Aston Villa two days earlier.

It was part of a fixture backlog that required them to play four games in seven days, but a part of that chaotic scheduling was caused by their own fans whose protests against their owners, the Glazers, meant their game against Liverpool had to be postponed.

What really mattered to Blues fans was that this well-deserved Leicester victory confirmed that we couldn't be caught with three games remaining. It was almost an action replay of the 2017-18 season when struggling West Brom won at United to hand us the title on a day we weren't playing football and Guardiola was playing golf.

But let's not dwell on Trafford's travails, let's focus on Etihad ecstasy.

In a campaign ravaged by Covid-19, we came out on top of the pile through sheer consistency and steely determination allied to the sheer genius of the best manager on the planet.

Of course, we had the best squad and probably the best backroom staff, but this was basically a triumph of mind over matter.

After virtually no pre-season because we were still playing Champions League games from 2019-20, our Premier League campaign got off to a terrible start, in part triggered by the disappointment of a dismal defeat in the CL quarter-final to a fairly modest Lyon side.

At one point in September, we had slumped to thirteenth in the table (with a game in hand) after being beaten 5-2 by Leicester, giving away an astonishing three penalties.

And then when Spurs staged their usual 'daylight robbery' at the Tottenham Hotspur Stadium in November, scoring two goals from their only two shots on target in a 2-0 success, City were still languishing in thirteenth spot and being written off by virtually every pundit.

Then West Brom held out against all the odds to take a 1-1 draw in a game where we failed to take our chances and it looked as though we would be looking for a top four place at the very best.

It was then that Pragmatic Pep took over. He fashioned wins over Southampton and Newcastle (Premier League) and Arsenal (League Cup) before lighting the blue touch paper against Chelsea as we outclassed the Pensioners with three goals in a devastating 16-minute spell.

That victory at Stamford Bridge was part of a 21-game unbeaten run across all competitions, which included 15 straight wins in the Premiership.

The passing style was the same, the possession stats similar, but the defensive frailties had been eradicated thanks to the acquisition of Ruben Dias and the re-emergence of John Stones.

There seemed no way through our central defensive pairing and with Kyle Walker working harder than ever and Ederson keeping clean sheet after clean sheet we were no longer vulnerable to sides who counter-attacked or tried to use pace over the top.

In midfield, Fernandinho was used sparingly to save his legs – his tactical fouling becoming almost an art form – and Rodri showed massive improvement from the season before.

Cancelo, after a poor first season, was given a free role in many games and looked good in most of them, while the unsung Zinchenko proved one of the 'finds' of the season even though he has been at the club since 2016.

Laporte lost his place after that defeat at Tottenham, but has come back strongly and is proving an able deputy in Pep's 'Rotation, Rotation, Rotation' programme.

There is almost an embarrassment of riches up front. Take your pick from the masterful Kevin De Bruyne, the influential Gündogan, the sheer youthful exuberance and talent that is Phil Foden, the revitalised Mahrez and the non-stop Bernardo.

There have, of course, been some disappointments, notably the iconic Aguero, who bids farewell to the club after ten seasons. Injury and illness have hampered his efforts and it is understood to have been the manager's decision not to extend his contract.

No City fan will ever forget what he has done for this club and I wish him well when he starts the twilight part of his career at Barcelona – thankfully he won't be playing in the colours of one of our Premier League rivals.

Without being able to rely on Aguero and not totally trusting in Jesus, who to be fair is often played as a false nine, Pep, in effect, re-invented the wheel, employing several other players as false nines, allowing his forwards to interchange with bewildering speed. It meant that centre-backs were virtually taken out of the equation; they simply had no one to mark. It worked a treat as results showed.

As with any big squad, there were a number of players who didn't come up to the mark. Sterling was one of them. He had a disappointing end to the campaign, appearing to have, temporarily at least, lost his touch. I'm sure he'll be back firing on all cylinders for us. His form in Euro 2020 was hugely encouraging.

Of the others, Ake and Torres haven't really hit the heights on a consistent level. The pair will no doubt be better with a second season at the club behind them. They certainly have the ability.

PEP'S SENSE OF HISTORY Guardiola dedicated the title win to "Colin Bell and his family". He added: "This has been a season and a Premier League title like no other. This was the hardest one. We will always remember this season for the way that we won. I am so proud to be the manager here and of this group of players."

FERNANDINHO SAID: "We will enjoy this moment and hope the fans do, too."

FRED IN THE RED Betfred's Fred Done got it spectacularly wrong in 1998 when he found himself £500,000 out of pocket after he paid out on United as League winners when they were 12 points clear of Arsenal, only for the Gunners to storm back and take the crown with two games to spare.

TREBLES ALL ROUND FOR PEP City landing the Premiership crown has ensured that Pep has won three league titles at each of the three clubs he has managed – Barcelona, Bayern Munich and the Blues.

ACKNOWLEDGMENTS

King of the Kippax fanzine, especially editors Dave & Sue Wallace; my brother Adrian for proof reading and some pictures; Paul Demby for his indefatigable statistic checking and proof reading.

SOURCES USED: *Manchester City a Complete Record 1887-1987* by Ray Goble (Breedon Books Sport); Colin *Bell – Reluctant Hero* by Colin Bell and Ian Cheeseman (Mainstream Publishing); *Us and Them* by Dave Wallace (King of the Kippax); *Little Book of Manchester City* by David Clayton (G2 Entertainment); *The Tipping Point* by Malcolm Gladwell (Abacus); clarets-mad.co.uk and many newspaper and club websites.

Also available:

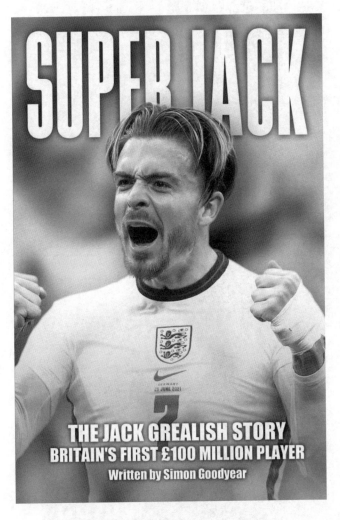

www.g2books.co.uk

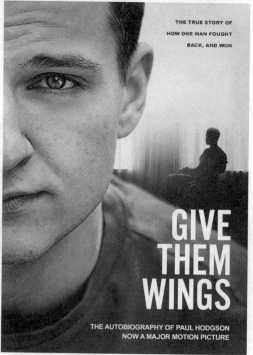